SIDE *by* SIDES

PRESTWICK HOUSE, INC.

JULIUS CAESAR

WILLIAM SHAKESPEARE

Shakespeare's text

on the left;

modern rendering

on the right.

PH
PRESTWICK HOUSE
INCORPORATED

P.O. Box 658 • Clayton, DE 19938
Tel: 1.800.932.4593
Web site: www.prestwickhouse.com

ISBN 978-1-58049-519-6

Table of Contents

DRAMATIS PERSONAE

JULIUS CAESAR, Roman statesman and general
OCTAVIUS, Triumvir after Caesar's death, later Augustus Caesar, first emperor of
    Rome
MARCUS ANTONIUS, general and friend of Caesar, a Triumvir after his death
LEPIDUS, third member of the Triumvirate
MARCUS BRUTUS, leader of the conspiracy against Caesar
CASSIUS, instigator of the conspiracy
CASCA,
TREBONIUS,
LIGARIUS, ⎫ conspirators against Caesar
DECIUS BRUTUS, ⎬
METELLUS CIMBER, ⎭
CINNA,
CALPURNIA, wife of Caesar
PORTIA, wife of Brutus
CICERO,
PUBLIUS, ⎫ senators
POPILIUS LENA, ⎭
FLAVIUS, tribune
MARULLUS, tribune
CATO,
LUCILIUS,
TITINIUS, ⎫ supporters of Brutus
MESSALA, ⎬
VOLUMNIUS, ⎭
ARTEMIDORUS, a teacher of rhetoric
CINNA, a poet
VARRO,
CLITUS,
CLAUDIUS, ⎫ servants to Brutus
STRATO, ⎬
LUCIUS, ⎭
DARDANIUS,
PINDARUS, servant to Cassius
Ghost of Caesar
A Soothsayer
A Poet
Senators, Citizens, Soldiers, Commoners, Messengers, and Servants

SCENE: Rome, the conspirators' camp near Sardis, and the plains of Philippi.

ACT I

SCENE 1
Rome. A street.

[Enter Flavius, Marullus, and certain Commoners.]

FLAVIUS: Hence! home, you idle creatures, get you home.
  Is this a holiday? What, know you not,
  Being mechanical, you ought not walk
  Upon a laboring day without the sign
5 Of your profession? Speak, what trade art thou?

FIRST COMMONER: Why, sir, a carpenter.

MARULLUS: Where is thy leather apron and thy rule?
  What dost thou with thy best apparel on?
  You, sir, what trade are you?

10 SEC. COMMONER: Truly, sir, in respect of a fine workman, I am
  but, as you would say, a cobbler.

MARULLUS: But what trade art thou? Answer me directly.

SECOND COMMONER: A trade, sir, that, I hope, I may use with a
  safe conscience, which is indeed, sir, a mender of bad soles.

15 MARULLUS: What trade, thou knave? Thou naughty knave, what
  trade?

ACT I

SCENE 1
Rome. A street.

[Enter Flavius, Marullus, and certain Commoners.]

FLAVIUS: *Away! Go home, you idle creatures. Is this a holiday? Don't you know that you should display the signs of your profession? Well, what trade do you practice?*

FIRST COMMONER: *Well, sir, I am carpenter.*

MARSULLUS: *Where is your leather apron and your ruler? Why do you dress in your best clothes? You, man, what is your trade?*

SECOND COMMONER: *Truly, sir, in comparison to a fine workman, I am only, as you would say, a cobbler.*

MARSULLUS: *But what trade are you? Answer me directly.*

SECOND COMMONER: *A trade, sir, that I hope I may use with a safe conscience. Indeed, sir, I am mender of bad soles.*

MARSULLUS: *What trade, you fool? You sly fool, what trade?*

SEC. COMMONER: Nay, I beseech you, sir, be not out with me; yet, if you be out, sir, I can mend you.

MARULLUS: What mean'st thou by that? Mend me, thou saucy fellow!

20   SEC. COMMONER: Why, sir, cobble you.

FLAVIUS: Thou art a cobbler, art thou?

SEC. COMMONER: Truly, Sir, all that I live by is with the awl; I meddle with no tradesman's matters, nor women's matters, but with awl. I am indeed, sir, a surgeon to old shoes; when they are in great danger, I recover them. As proper men as
25   ever trod upon neats-leather have gone upon my handiwork.

FLAVIUS: But wherefore art not in thy shop today?
Why dost thou lead these men about the streets?

SEC. COMMONER: Truly, sir, to wear out their shoes, to get myself into more work. But indeed, sir, we make holiday, to see
30   Caesar and to rejoice in his triumph.

MARULLUS: Wherefore rejoice? What conquest brings he home?
What tributaries follow him to Rome,
To grace in captive bonds his chariot-wheels?
You blocks, you stones, you worse than senseless things!
35   O you hard hearts, you cruel men of Rome,
Knew you not Pompey? Many a time and oft
Have you climb'd up to walls and battlements,
To towers and windows, yea, to chimney tops,
Your infants in your arms, and there have sat
40   The live-long day with patient expectation
To see great Pompey pass the streets of Rome.
And when you saw his chariot but appear,
Have you not made an universal shout,
That Tiber trembled underneath her banks
45   To hear the replication of your sounds

SECOND COMMONER: *I pray you, sir, do not be mad at me. Yet, sir, if you are mad, I can mend you.*

MARSULLUS: *What do you mean by that? Mend me, you silly fellow!*

SECOND COMMONER: *Why, sir, cobble you.*

FLAVIUS: *You are a cobbler, are you?*

SECOND COMMONER: *Yes, sir, all that I live by is with my awl. I meddle with no man's matters, nor woman's matters, but with awl. I am indeed, sir, a surgeon to old shoes. When they are in great danger, I mend them. The most proper men who have ever walked upon neatly trimmed leather, walk upon my handiwork.*

FLAVIUS: *But why are you not in your shop today? Why do you lead these men about the streets?*

SECOND COMMONER: *Truly, sir, I wear out their shoes to get myself more work. But indeed, sir, we make holiday to see Caesar and to rejoice in his triumph.*

MARSULLUS: *Why do you rejoice? What conquest does he bring home to Rome? What bound captives follow him to grace his chariot wheels? You blocks, you stones, you worse than senseless things! O, you hard hearts, you cruel men of Rome. Did you not know Pompey? Time and time again you climbed up to the walls and battlements, to towers and windows—even to chimney tops, with your infants in your arms. There you have sat the entire day, with patient expectation, to see great Pompey pass in the streets of Rome. When you only saw his chariot appear, did you not make such a loud shout that the river trembled underneath her banks and the sound reached its far side? And now you put on your best attire. And call out for a holiday. And now you strew flowers in his way who comes in triumph over Pompey's body. Be gone! Run to your houses, fall upon your knees, pray to the gods to stop the plague that must now fall on your ingratitude.*

Made in her concave shores?
And do you now put on your best attire?
And do you now cull out a holiday?
And do you now strew flowers in his way
50   That comes in triumph over Pompey's blood?
Be gone!
Run to your houses, fall upon your knees,
Pray to the gods to intermit the plague
That needs must light on this ingratitude.

55   FLAVIUS: Go, go, good countrymen, and, for this fault,
Assemble all the poor men of your sort,
Draw them to Tiber banks, and weep your tears
Into the channel, till the lowest stream
Do kiss the most exalted shores of all.
[Exeunt all Commoners.]
60   See, whether their basest metal be not moved;
They vanish tongue-tied in their guiltiness.
Go you down that way towards the Capitol;
This way will I. Disrobe the images,
If you do find them deck'd with ceremonies.

65   MARULLUS: May we do so?
You know it is the feast of Lupercal.

FLAVIUS: It is no matter; let no images
Be hung with Caesar's trophies. I'll about,
And drive away the vulgar from the streets;
70   So do you too, where you perceive them thick.
These growing feathers pluck'd from Caesar's wing
Will make him fly an ordinary pitch,
Who else would soar above the view of men
And keep us all in servile fearfulness.   *[Exeunt.]*

FLAVIUS: Go, go, good countrymen, and for this sin assemble all the poor men like you. Bring them to the river's banks and weep tears into its channel until the smallest stream kisses the most exalted shores of all.
                              [Exit all the Commoners.]
See how we have changed their hearts; they vanish tongue-tied with their guilt. Go down that way towards the Capitol. I will go this way, and we should both remove any festival banners that we find on Caesar's statues.

MARSULLUS: May we do so? You know it is the feast of Lupercal.

FLAVIUS: It is no matter; no images should be hung with Caesar's trophies. I'll go and drive away the commoners from the streets. Do likewise wherever you see them in a crowd. Removing these decorations will dampen Ceasar's image and hopefully keep us from his slavery.
                              [Exit.]

SCENE 2
A public place.

[Flourish. Enter Caesar; Antony, for the course; Calpurnia, Portia, Decius, Cicero, Brutus, Cassius, and Casca; a great crowd following, among them a Soothsayer.]

CAESAR: Calpurnia!

CASCA: Peace, ho! Caesar speaks.
                              [Music ceases.]

CAESAR: Calpurnia!

CALPURNIA: Here, my lord.

5   CAESAR: Stand you directly in Antonio's way,
        When he doth run his course. Antonio!

ANTONY: Caesar, my lord?

CAESAR: Forget not, in your speed, Antonio,
        To touch Calpurnia, for our elders say,
10   The barren, touched in this holy chase,
        Shake off their sterile curse.

ANTONY: I shall remember.
        When Caesar says "Do this," it is perform'd.

CAESAR: Set on, and leave no ceremony out.   *[Flourish.]*

15   SOOTHSAYER: Caesar!

CAESAR: Ha! Who calls?

CASCA: Bid every noise be still. Peace yet again!

SCENE 2
A public place.

[Flourish. Enter Caesar; Antony, for the course; Calpurnia, Portia, Decius, Cicero, Brutus, Cassius, and Casca; a great crowd follows, among them a Soothsayer.]

CAESAR: *Calpurnia!*

CASCA: *Quiet, there! Caesar speaks.*
                    [Music ceases.]

CAESAR: *Calpurnia!*

CALPURNIA: *Here, my lord.*

CAESAR: *Stand directly in Antonio's path when he runs by. Antonio!*

ANTONY: *Caesar, my lord?*

CAESAR: *Do not forget in your run, Antonio, to touch Calpurnia. Our elders say that the barren, touched in this holy chase, will shake off their sterile curse.*

ANTONY: *I shall remember. When Caesar says, "Do this," it is done.*

CAESAR: *Go now, and leave no ceremony out.*   [Flourish.]

SOOTHSAYER: *Caesar!*

CAESAR: *Ha! who calls?*

CASCA: *Bid every noise be still. Quiet, everyone!*

CAESAR: Who is it in the press that calls on me?
    I hear a tongue, shriller than all the music,
20   Cry "Caesar." Speak, Caesar is turn'd to hear.

SOOTHSAYER: Beware the ides of March.

CAESAR: What man is that?

BRUTUS: A soothsayer bids you beware the ides of March.

CAESAR: Set him before me; let me see his face.

25   CASSIUS: Fellow, come from the throng; look upon Caesar.

CAESAR: What say'st thou to me now? Speak once again.

SOOTHSAYER: Beware the ides of March.

CAESAR: He is a dreamer; let us leave him. Pass.
                [Exeunt all but Brutus and Cassius.]

CASSIUS: Will you go see the order of the course?

30   BRUTUS: Not I.

CASSIUS: I pray you, do.

BRUTUS: I am not gamesome; I do lack some part
    Of that quick spirit that is in Antony.
    Let me not hinder, Cassius, your desires;
35   I'll leave you.

CASSIUS: Brutus, I do observe you now of late;
    I have not from your eyes that gentleness
    And show of love as I was wont to have;
    You bear too stubborn and too strange a hand
40   Over your friend that loves you.

CAESAR: *Who is it in the crowd that calls. Who calls me? I hear a tongue, shriller than all the music, cry "Caesar." Speak, Caesar is turned to hear you.*

SOOTHSAYER: *Beware the ides of March.*

CAESAR: *What man is that?*

BRUTUS: *A soothsayer asks you to beware of the fifteenth of March.*

CAESAR: *Set him before me. Let me see his face.*

CASSIUS: *Fellow, come from the throng. Look upon Caesar.*

CAESAR: *What do you have to say now? Speak once again.*

SOOTHSAYER: *Beware the ides of March.*

CAESAR: *He is a dreamer; let us leave him. Pass.*
                    [Exit all but Brutus and Cassius.]

CASSIUS: *Will you go to see the race?*

BRUTUS: *Not I.*

CASSIUS: *I pray you, do go.*

BRUTUS: *I am not into games. I do lack some part of that quick spirit that is in Antony. Let me not hinder your desires; I'll leave you.*

CASSIUS: *Brutus, I have observed you lately. I have not received from your eyes that gentleness and show of love that I used to have. You seem too cool and distant with a friend who loves you.*

15

BRUTUS: Cassius,
Be not deceived; if I have veil'd my look,
I turn the trouble of my countenance
Merely upon myself. Vexed I am
45   Of late with passions of some difference,
Conceptions only proper to myself,
Which give some soil perhaps to my behaviors;
But let not therefore my good friends be grieved—
Among which number, Cassius, be you one—
50   Nor construe any further my neglect
Than that poor Brutus with himself at war
Forgets the shows of love to other men.

CASSIUS: Then, Brutus, I have much mistook your passion,
By means whereof this breast of mine hath buried
55   Thoughts of great value, worthy cogitations.
Tell me, good Brutus, can you see your face?

BRUTUS: No, Cassius, for the eye sees not itself
But by reflection, by some other things.

CASSIUS: 'Tis just,
60   And it is very much lamented, Brutus,
That you have no such mirrors as will turn
Your hidden worthiness into your eye
That you might see your shadow. I have heard
Where many of the best respect in Rome,
65   Except immortal Caesar, speaking of Brutus,
And groaning underneath this age's yoke,
Have wish'd that noble Brutus had his eyes.

BRUTUS: Into what dangers would you lead me, Cassius,
That you would have me seek into myself
70   For that which is not in me?

CASSIUS: Therefore, good Brutus, be prepared to hear,
And since you know you cannot see yourself
So well as by reflection, I your glass

BRUTUS: Cassius, be not deceived. If I have veiled my look, I turn the trouble of my looks entirely upon myself. I am preoccupied of late with different passions—ideas proper only to myself, which give some reason perhaps for my behaviors. But do not let any of my good friends be upset—among which number, Cassius, you are one—nor read anything into my neglect other than that poor Brutus wars with himself and forgets to show his love to other men.

CASSIUS: Then, Brutus, I have much mistaken your passions and in so doing I have buried thoughts of great value, that are worthy of your thinking. Tell me, good Brutus, can you see your face?

BRUTUS: No, Cassius, for the eye does not see itself but only its reflection.

CASSIUS: It is so. But it is very much lamented, Brutus, that you have no such mirrors that will turn your hidden worthiness into your eye so that you might see yourself as others see you. I have heard many respected men in Rome, except immortal Caesar, speak of Brutus and groaning under the burden of the present, wish that noble Brutus had eyes to see what was happening.

BRUTUS: Into what dangers would you lead me, Cassius, that you would have me look into myself for something that is not there?

CASSIUS: Therefore, good Brutus, be prepared to hear. Since you know you cannot see yourself except in reflection, I will be your mirror that you may use to discover the self of which you don't know. And be not

Will modestly discover to yourself
75 That of yourself which you yet know not of.
And be not jealous on me, gentle Brutus;
Were I a common laugher, or did use
To stale with ordinary oaths my love
To every new protester, if you know
80 That I do fawn on men and hug them hard
And after scandal them, or if you know
That I profess myself in banqueting
To all the rout, then hold me dangerous.
[Flourish and shout.]

BRUTUS: What means this shouting? I do fear the people
85 Choose Caesar for their king.

CASSIUS: Ay, do you fear it?
Then must I think you would not have it so.

BRUTUS: I would not, Cassius, yet I love him well.
But wherefore do you hold me here so long?
90 What is it that you would impart to me?
If it be aught toward the general good,
Set honor in one eye and death i' the other
And I will look on both indifferently.
For let the gods so speed me as I love
95 The name of honor more than I fear death.

CASSIUS: I know that virtue to be in you, Brutus,
As well as I do know your outward favor.
Well, honor is the subject of my story.
I cannot tell what you and other men
100 Think of this life, but, for my single self, •
I had as lief not be as live to be
In awe of such a thing as I myself.
I was born free as Caesar, so were you;
We both have fed as well, and we can both
105 Endure the winter's cold as well as he.
For once, upon a raw and gusty day,

18

suspicious of me, gentle Brutus. If you know me to be a common joke-
ster or one to swear oaths of love to every new solemn proclamation, or
one that fawns on men, hugs them hard and later speaks ill of them, then
hold me dangerous.   [Flourish and shout]

BRUTUS: What means this shouting? I am afraid the people have chosen
Caesar for their king.

CASSIUS: Oh, do you fear it? I think you do not want this to happen.

BRUTUS: I would not, Cassius, yet I love Caesar well. But why do you hold
me here so long? What is it that you would tell me? If it is for the gen-
eral good, set honor and death before me, and I will look on both indif-
ferently. For I swear by the gods, that I love the name of honor more than
I fear death.

CASSIUS: I know that virtue is in you, Brutus, as well as I know your physi-
cal features. Well, honor is the subject of my story. I cannot tell what
you and other men think of this life but, for myself, I don't want to live
in awe of someone who is no better than I. I was born free just like
Caesar and so were you. We both have eaten just as well, and we can
both endure the winter's cold as well as he. Once, upon a raw and gusty
day, while the troubled Tiber was rolling against her shores, Caesar said
to me, "Do you dare, Cassius, to leap with me into this angry flood and
swim to yonder point?" Upon that word, dressed as I was, I plunged in
and bade him follow. Indeed, so he did. The river roared and we did fight
it with our muscles, throwing it aside and stemming it with our compet-

19

The troubled Tiber chafing with her shores,
Caesar said to me, "Darest thou, Cassius, now
Leap in with me into this angry flood
110   And swim to yonder point?" Upon the word,
Accoutred as I was, I plunged in
And bade him follow. So indeed he did.
The torrent roar'd, and we did buffet it
With lusty sinews, throwing it aside
115   And stemming it with hearts of controversy.
But ere we could arrive the point proposed,
Caesar cried, "Help me, Cassius, or I sink!"
I, as Aeneas our great ancestor
Did from the flames of Troy upon his shoulder
120   The old Anchises bear, so from the waves of Tiber
Did I the tired Caesar. And this man
Is now become a god, and Cassius is
A wretched creature, and must bend his body
If Caesar carelessly but nod on him.
125   He had a fever when he was in Spain,
And when the fit was on him, I did mark
How he did shake. 'Tis true, this god did shake;
His coward lips did from their color fly,
And that same eye whose bend doth awe the world
130   Did lose his luster. I did hear him groan.
Ay, and that tongue of his that bade the Romans
Mark him and write his speeches in their books,
Alas, it cried, "Give me some drink, Titinius,"
As a sick girl. Ye gods! It doth amaze me
135   A man of such a feeble temper should
So get the start of the majestic world
And bear the palm alone.   *[Shout. Flourish.]*

BRUTUS: Another general shout!
I do believe that these applauses are
140   For some new honors that are heap'd on Caesar.

CASSIUS: Why, man, he doth bestride the narrow world
Like a Colossus, and we petty men

20

itive hearts. But before we could arrive at the proposed point, Caesar cried, "Help me, Cassius—I sink!" Just as Aeneas, our great ancestor, carried Anchises from the flames of Troy upon his shoulder, so I from the waves of the Tiber did carry the tired Caesar. And this man is now a god, and Cassius is a wretched creature who must bend his body if Caesar merely nods towards him. He had a fever when he was in Spain; and when the fit was on him, I did see how he did shake. It is true. This god did shake and his lips grew pale. That same eye whose glare awes the world did lose his color. I did hear him groan. That tongue which ordered the Romans to take him into account cried, "Give me some drink, Titinius," as if he were a sick girl. Oh, gods, it does amaze me that a man of such a feeble temperament should gain this majestic world and rule Rome alone.   [Shout. Flourish.]

BRUTUS: Another general shout! I do believe that these cheers are for some new honors which are heaped on Caesar.

CASSIUS: Why, man, he straddles the narrow world like a Colossus; and we petty men walk under his huge legs and peep about to find our own

Walk under his huge legs and peep about
To find ourselves dishonorable graves.
145 Men at some time are masters of their fates:
The fault, dear Brutus, is not in our stars,
But in ourselves, that we are underlings.
Brutus, and Caesar: what should be in that Caesar?
Why should that name be sounded more than yours?
150 Write them together, yours is as fair a name;
Sound them, it doth become the mouth as well;
Weigh them, it is as heavy; conjure with 'em,
Brutus will start a spirit as soon as Caesar.
Now, in the names of all the gods at once,
155 Upon what meat doth this our Caesar feed
That he is grown so great? Age, thou art shamed!
Rome, thou hast lost the breed of noble bloods!
When went there by an age since the great flood
But it was famed with more than with one man?
160 When could they say till now that talk'd of Rome
That her wide walls encompass'd but one man?
Now is it Rome indeed, and room enough,
When there is in it but one only man.
O, you and I have heard our fathers say
165 There was a Brutus once that would have brook'd
The eternal devil to keep his state in Rome
As easily as a king.

BRUTUS: That you do love me, I am nothing jealous;
What you would work me to, I have some aim.
175 How I have thought of this and of these times,
I shall recount hereafter; for this present,
I would not, so with love I might entreat you,
Be any further moved. What you have said
I will consider; what you have to say
180 I will with patience hear, and find a time
Both meet to hear and answer such high things.
Till then, my noble friend, chew upon this:
Brutus had rather be a villager
Than to repute himself a son of Rome

dishonorable graves. Men at times are masters of their own fates. The fault, dear Brutus, is not in our stars but in ourselves if we act like underlings. Brutus and Caesar. What is special about "Caesar"? Why should that name be sounded more than yours? Write them together; yours is as fair a name. Say them; yours rolls off the tongue as nicely. Weigh them; yours is as heavy. Conjure with them; "Brutus" will start a spirit just as easily as "Caesar." Now, in the names of all the gods, upon what meat does this Caesar feed since he is grown so great? Age, you are shameful! Rome, you have lost your breed of nobles. Since time began, there has not been an age dominated by such a man. Before this they talked of Rome, and not the feats of just a single man. Now there is room enough for only one man. You and I have heard our fathers say that there once was a Brutus who would have endured the devil in Rome, rather than have a king.

BRUTUS: *I do not doubt that you do love me. I guess what you are hinting at. I have thought of this and of these times often, and I shall speak more of this later. For the present, though, I ask you as a good friend not to press me further. What you have said I will consider; what you have to yet say, I will hear with patience and find a time to both hear and answer such important thoughts. Until then, my noble friend, chew upon this— Brutus would rather be a villager than to call himself a son of Rome under the hard conditions which this time is likely to lay upon us.*

185   Under these hard conditions as this time
        Is like to lay upon us.

CASSIUS: I am glad that my weak words
        Have struck but thus much show of fire from Brutus.

[Approach Caesar and his Train.]

BRUTUS: The games are done, and Caesar is returning.

190   CASSIUS: As they pass by, pluck Casca by the sleeve,
        And he will, after his sour fashion, tell you
        What hath proceeded worthy note today.

BRUTUS: I will do so. But, look you, Cassius,
        The angry spot doth glow on Caesar's brow,
195   And all the rest look like a chidden train:
        Calpurnia's cheek is pale, and Cicero
        Looks with such ferret and such fiery eyes
        As we have seen him in the Capitol,
        Being cross'd in conference by some senators.

200   CASSIUS: Casca will tell us what the matter is.

CAESAR: *[Calls out.]* Antonio!

ANTONY: Caesar?

CAESAR: Let me have men about me that are fat,
        Sleek-headed men, and such as sleep o' nights:
205   Yond Cassius has a lean and hungry look;
        He thinks too much; such men are dangerous.

ANTONY: Fear him not, Caesar; he's not dangerous;
        He is a noble Roman and well given.

CAESAR: Would he were fatter! But I fear him not,
210   Yet if my name were liable to fear,

24

CASSIUS: *I am glad that my weak words have struck so well as to bring a show of fire from Brutus.*

[Approach Caesar and his Train.]

BRUTUS: *The games are done, and Caesar is returning.*

CASSIUS: *As they pass by, pluck Casca by the sleeve; and he will, after his sour fashion, tell you what important things happened today.*

BRUTUS: *I will do so. But, look, Cassius, how the angry spot glows on Caesar's brow and how all the others look like scolded men. Calpurnia's cheek is pale, and Cicero looks with such angry and fiery eyes as we have seen him in the Capitol when he was crossed in conference by some senators.*

CASSIUS: *Casca will tell us what is the matter.*

CAESAR: [Calls out.] *Antony!*

ANTONY: *Caesar?*

CAESAR: *Let me have men about me that are fat, sleek-headed men, and such as those who sleep at night. That Cassius has a lean and hungry look; he thinks too much—such men are dangerous.*

ANTONY: *Fear him not, Caesar; he's not dangerous; he is a noble Roman and well devoted.*

CAESAR: *I wish he were fatter! I don't fear him. But if my name were liable to fear, I do not know the man I should avoid as quickly as that slender*

I do not know the man I should avoid
So soon as that spare Cassius. He reads much,
He is a great observer, and he looks
Quite through the deeds of men. He loves no plays,
215   As thou dost, Antony; he hears no music;
Seldom he smiles, and smiles in such a sort
As if he mock'd himself, and scorn'd his spirit
That could be moved to smile at any thing.
Such men as he be never at heart's ease
220   Whiles they behold a greater than themselves,
And therefore are they very dangerous.
I rather tell thee what is to be fear'd
Than what I fear, for always I am Caesar.
Come on my right hand, for this ear is deaf,
225   And tell me truly what thou think'st of him.
> *[Sennet. Exeunt Caesar and all his Train but Casca.]*

CASCA: You pull'd me by the cloak; would you speak with me?

BRUTUS: Ay, Casca, tell us what hath chanced today,
That Caesar looks so sad.

CASCA: Why, you were with him, were you not?

230   BRUTUS: I should not then ask Casca what had chanced.

CASCA: Why, there was a crown offered him, and being offered
him: he put it by with the back of his hand, thus, and then
the people fell a-shouting.

BRUTUS: What was the second noise for?

235   CASCA: Why, for that too.

CASSIUS: They shouted thrice. What was the last cry for?

CASCA: Why, for that too.

Cassius. He reads much; he is a great observer, and he looks quite through the deeds of men. He doesn't like plays as you do, Antony; he listens to no music. He seldom smiles, and smiles in such a way as if he mocked himself and scorned his better spirit which could be moved to smile at anything. Such men as he are never content while they behold someone greater than themselves. Therefore, they are very dangerous. I tell you what is to be feared rather than what I fear. I am always Caesar. Come to my right side, for this ear is deaf, and tell me what you really think of him.

[Sennet. Exit Caesar and all his followers but Casca.]

CASCA: *You pulled me by my cloak; do you need to speak with me?*

BRUTUS: *Yes, Casca, tell us what has occurred today that Caesar looks so serious.*

CASCA: *Why, weren't you with him?*

BRUTUS: *If I had been, I would not then be asking you what happened.*

CASCA: *Why, there was a crown offered to him. Being offered, he pushed it away with the back of his hand,* [Makes dismissive motion.] *thusly; and then the people began to shout.*

BRUTUS: *Why the second noise?*

CASCA: *Why, for that, too.*

CASSIUS: *They shouted three times. What was the last cry for?*

CASCA: *Why, for that, too.*

BRUTUS: Was the crown offered him thrice?

CASCA: Ay, marry, wast, and he put it by thrice, every time gen-
240   tler than other, and at every putting by mine honest neighbors
shouted.

CASSIUS: Who offered him the crown?

CASCA: Why, Antony.

BRUTUS: Tell us the manner of it, gentle Casca.

245   CASCA: I can as well be hang'd as tell the manner of it. It was
mere foolery; I did not mark it. I saw Mark Antony offer him
a crown, yet 'twas not a crown neither, 'twas one of these
coronets and, as I told you, he put it by once. But for all that,
to my thinking, he would fain have had it. Then he offered it
250   to him again; then he put it by again. But, to my thinking, he
was very loath to lay his fingers off it. And then he offered it
the third time; he put it the third time by; and still as he
refused it, the rabblement hooted and clapped their chopped
hands and threw up their sweaty nightcaps and uttered such a
255   deal of stinking breath because Caesar refused the crown, that
it had almost choked Caesar, for he swounded and fell down
at it. And for mine own part, I durst not laugh for fear of
opening my lips and receiving the bad air.

CASSIUS: But, soft, I pray you, what, did Caesars swound?

260   CASCA: He fell down in the market-place and foamed at mouth
and was speechless.

BRUTUS: 'Tis very like: he hath the falling sickness.

CASSIUS: No, Caesar hath it not, but you, and I,
And honest Casca, we have the falling sickness.

BRUTUS: *Was the crown offered to him three times?*

CASCA: *Yes, truly, it was; and he pushed it away three times, but every time gentler than the previous. At every instance my honest neighbors shouted.*

CASSIUS: *Who offered him the crown?*

CASCA: *Why, Antony.*

BRUTUS: *Tell us the manner of it, noble Casca.*

CASCA: *I could just as easily be hanged as tell the manner of it—it was mere foolishness—I did not pay that much attention. I saw Mark Antony offer him a crown—yet it was not really a crown but only one of these little crowns fashioned from laurel leaves. And, as I told you, he pushed it away once. But for all that, to my thinking, he really wanted to have it. Then Antony offered it to him again; then, he refused it again. But, to my thinking, he was very reluctant to keep his fingers off of it. And then Antony offered it the third time; he put it away the third time. As he refused it, the rabble hooted and clapped their chapped hands and threw up their sweaty nightcaps; they uttered such a deal of stinking breath, because Caesar refused the crown, that it almost choked Caesar. He fainted and fell down at it. For my own part, I could not laugh for fear of opening my lips and receiving the bad air.*

CASSIUS: *But, easy, I pray you—did Caesar faint?*

CASCA: *He fell down in the marketplace and foamed at the mouth and was speechless.*

BRUTUS: *It is very likely, since he has epilepsy, the falling sickness.*

CASSIUS: *No, Caesar does not have it. But you and I, and honest Casca, we have the falling sickness.*

265 CASCA: I know not what you mean by that, but I am sure Caesar
    fell down. If the tag-rag people did not clap him and hiss him
    according as he pleased and displeased them, as they use to
    do the players in the theatre, I am no true man.

270 BRUTUS: What said he when he came unto himself?

    CASCA: Marry, before he fell down, when he perceived the com-
    mon herd was glad he refused the crown, he plucked me ope
    his doublet and offered them his throat to cut. An had been a
    man of any occupation, if I would not have taken him at a
275 word, I would I might go to hell among the rogues. And so he
    fell. When he came to himself again, he said, if he had done
    or said any thing amiss, he desired their worships to think it
    was his infirmity. Three or four wenches, where I stood cried,
    "Alas, good soul!" and forgave him with all their hearts. But
280 there's no heed to be taken of them; if Caesar had stabbed
    their mothers, they would have done no less.

    BRUTUS: And after that, he came, thus sad, away?

    CASCA: Ay.

    CASSIUS: Did Cicero say anything?

285 CASCA: Ay, he spoke Greek.

    CASSIUS: To what effect?

    CASCA: Nay, an I tell you that, I'll ne'er look you i' the face again;
    but those that understood him smiled at one another and
    shook their heads; but for mine own part, it was Greek to me.
290 I could tell you more news too: Marullus and Flavius, for
    pulling scarfs off Caesar's images, are put to silence. Fare you
    well. There was more foolery yet, if could remember it.

    CASSIUS: Will you sup with me tonight, Casca?

CASCA: *I do not know what you mean by that. But I am sure Caesar fell down. If the ragtag people did not clap and hiss at him whenever he pleased and displeased them, as they do for the players in the theatre, I am no honest man.*

BRUTUS: *What did he say when he came to his senses?*

CASCA: *Well, before he fell down, when he perceived the common herd was glad he refused the crown, he plucked open his tunic and offered them his throat to cut.* [With heavy sarcasm.] *If I had been a lowly workingman I would have taken him at his word and been moved to do as he commanded. Then he fell. When he came to himself again, he said he desired them to think it was only his infirmity if he had done or said anything amiss. Three or four girls where I stood cried, "Alas, good soul!" and forgave him with all their hearts. There's no sense in that. If Caesar had stabbed their mothers, they would have forgiven him.*

BRUTUS: *And after that did he come away sadly?*

CASCA: *Yes.*

CASSIUS: *Did Cicero say anything?*

CASCA: *Yes, he spoke Greek.*

CASSIUS: *To what effect?*

CASCA: *If you want an honest answer, don't look to me. But those that understood him smiled at one another and shook their heads. For my part, it was Greek to me. I could tell you more news, too. For pulling decorations off Caesar's images, Marullus and Flavius are silenced. Farewell. There was even more foolery if I could only remember it.*

CASSIUS: *Will you eat with me tonight, Casca?*

CASCA: No, I am promised forth.

295 CASSIUS: Will you dine with me tomorrow?

CASCA: Ay, if I be alive, and your mind hold, and your dinner
worth the eating.

CASSIUS: Good, I will expect you.

CASCA: Do so, farewell, both.   *[Exit.]*

300 BRUTUS: What a blunt fellow is this grown to be!
He was quick mettle when he went to school.

CASSIUS: So is he now in execution
Of any bold or noble enterprise,
However he puts on this tardy form.
305 This rudeness is a sauce to his good wit,
Which gives men stomach to digest his words
With better appetite.

BRUTUS: And so it is. For this time I will leave you.
Tomorrow, if you please to speak with me,
310 I will come home to you, or, if you will,
Come home to me and I will wait for you.

CASSIUS: I will do so. Till then, think of the world.
[Exit Brutus.]
Well, Brutus, thou art noble; yet, I see
Thy honorable metal may be wrought
315 From that it is disposed; therefore it is meet
That noble minds keep ever with their likes;
For who so firm that cannot be seduced?
Caesar doth bear me hard, but he loves Brutus.
If I were Brutus now and he were Cassius,
320 He should not humor me. I will this night,
In several hands, in at his windows throw,
As if they came from several citizens,

CASCA: *No, I have a prior engagement.*

CASSIUS: *Will you dine with me tomorrow?*

CASCA: *Ay, if I am alive, and you hold a similar mind, and your dinner is worth eating.*

CASSIUS: *Good. I will expect you.*

CASCA: *Do so. Farewell to both of you.*   [Exit.]

BRUTUS: *What a blunt fellow he has grown to be! He was high-spirited when he went to school.*

CASSIUS: *He is now in agreement with any bold or noble enterprise, no matter how late he is in agreeing. This rudeness is a sauce to his good intelligence, which gives men stomach to digest his words with a better appetite.*

BRUTUS: *So it is. Now, I will leave you. Tomorrow, if you please, speak with me. I will come to your home; or, if you would rather, come to mine, and I will wait for you.*

CASSIUS: *I will do so. Until then, think of the state of the world.*
                                    [Exit Brutus.]
Well, Brutus, you are noble. Yet, I see your honorable mettle may be twisted into another form. It is well that noble minds keep ever with their own kind. But who is so firm that he cannot be seduced? Caesar holds a grudge against me, but he loves Brutus. If I were Brutus now and he were Cassius, he should not persuade me. I will this night throw letters written in various handwritings into his windows. All the writings will be of the great opinion in which Rome holds his name. Each will touch on Caesar's ambition. After this, let Caesar feel secure, because we will shake him or endure worse days.
                                    [Exit.]

Writings, all tending to the great opinion
That Rome holds of his name, wherein obscurely
325   Caesar's ambition shall be glanced at.
And after this let Caesar seat him sure;
For we will shake him, or worse days endure.

[Exit.]

SCENE 3
A street. Thunder and lightning.

[Enter, from opposite sides, Casca, with his sword drawn, and Cicero.]

CICERO: Good even, Casca. Brought you Caesar home?
    Why are you breathless, and why stare you so?

CASCA: Are not you moved, when all the sway of earth
    Shakes like a thing unfirm? O Cicero,
5   I have seen tempests, when the scolding winds
    Have rived the knotty oaks, and I have seen
    The ambitious ocean swell and rage and foam,
    To be exalted with the threatening clouds,
    But never till tonight, never till now,
10   Did I go through a tempest dropping fire.
    Either there is a civil strife in heaven,
    Or else the world too saucy with the gods
    Incenses them to send destruction.

CICERO: Why, saw you anything more wonderful?

15   CASCA: A common slave—you know him well by sight—
    Held up his left hand, which did flame and burn
    Like twenty torches join'd, and yet his hand
    Not sensible of fire remain'd unscorch'd.
    Besides—I ha' not since put up my sword—

SCENE 3
A street. Thunder and lightning.

[Enter, from opposite sides, Casca, with his sword drawn, and Cicero.]

CICERO: *Good evening, Casca. Did you accompany Caesar home? Why are you breathless, and why do you stare so?*

CASCA: *Are you not moved when all the order of the earth shakes like an unfirm thing? Oh, Cicero, I have seen storms where the scolding winds have split old oaks, and I have seen the ambitious ocean swell and rage and foam to be coupled with threatening clouds; but never until tonight, never till now, did I go through a storm which dropped fire. Either there is a civil war in heaven, or else the saucy world incenses the gods and causes them to send destruction to the earth.*

CICERO: *Well, did you see anything more bizarre?*

CASCA: *A common slave—you know him well by sight—held up his left hand, which flamed and burned like twenty torches joined together, and yet his hand remained unburned. Further, I have not since then put my sword in its scabbard because I saw a lion across from the Capitol. It glared upon me and went sullenly by without even attacking me. There*

20   Against the Capitol I met a lion,
          Who glazed upon me and went surly by
          Without annoying me: and there were drawn
          Upon a heap a hundred ghastly women
          Transformed with their fear, who swore they saw
25   Men all in fire walk up and down the streets.
          And yesterday the bird of night did sit
          Even at noon-day upon the market-place,
          Howling and shrieking. When these prodigies
          Do so conjointly meet, let not men say
30   "These are their reasons; they are natural:"
          For, I believe, they are portentous things
          Unto the climate that they point upon.

CICERO: Indeed, it is a strange-disposed time;
          But men may construe things after their fashion,
35   Clean from the purpose of the things themselves.
          Come Caesar to the Capitol tomorrow?

CASCA: He doth; for he did bid Antonius
          Send word to you he would be there tomorrow.

CICERO: Good then, Casca. This disturbed sky
40   Is not to walk in.

CASCA: Farewell, Cicero.   *[Exit Cicero.]*

[Enter Cassius.]

CASSIUS: Who's there?

CASCA: A Roman.

CASSIUS: Casca, by your voice.

45   CASCA: Your ear is good. Cassius, what night is this!

CASSIUS: A very pleasing night to honest men.

were at least a hundred ghastly women huddling in fear who swore they saw men all in fire walk up and down the streets. And yesterday at noon the owl sat in the market-place, hooting and shrieking. When these startling events appear simultaneously, do not let men say, "These are reasonable—they are natural." I believe these events foretell things which will be terrible for our future.

CICERO: *Indeed, it is a strangely disposed time. But men may twist things in their own fashion and gather what they wish from them. Does Caesar come to the Capitol tomorrow?*

CASCA: *He does, for he bid Antonio to send word to you that he would be there tomorrow.*

CICERO: *Good then, Casca. This stormy sky is not to walk in.*

CASCA: *Farewell, Cicero.*　　　　[Exit Cicero.]

[Enter Cassius.]

CASSIUS: *Who's there?*

CASCA: *A Roman.*

CASSIUS: *By your voice, it is Casca.*

CASCA: *Your ear is good, Cassius. What a night this is!*

CASSIUS: *A very pleasing night to honest men.*

CASCA: Who ever knew the heavens menace so?

CASSIUS: Those that have known the earth so full of faults.
    For my part, I have walk'd about the streets,
50   Submitting me unto the perilous night,
    And thus unbraced, Casca, as you see,
    Have bared my bosom to the thunder-stone;
    And when the cross blue lightning seem'd to open
    The breast of heaven, I did present myself
55   Even in the aim and very flash of it.

CASCA: But wherefore did you so much tempt the heavens?
    It is the part of men to fear and tremble
    When the most mighty gods by tokens send
    Such dreadful heralds to astonish us.

60   CASSIUS: You are dull, Casca, and those sparks of life
    That should be in a Roman you do want,
    Or else you use not. You look pale and gaze
    And put on fear and cast yourself in wonder,
    To see the strange impatience of the heavens.
65   But if you would consider the true cause
    Why all these fires, why all these gliding ghosts,
    Why birds and beasts from quality and kind,
    Why old men fool, and children calculate,
    Why all these things change from their ordinance,
70   Their natures and preformed faculties,
    To monstrous quality, why, you shall find
    That heaven hath infused them with these spirits
    To make them instruments of fear and warning
    Unto some monstrous state.
75   Now could I, Casca, name to thee a man
    Most like this dreadful night,
    That thunders, lightens, opens graves, and roars
    As doth the lion in the Capitol,
    A man no mightier than thyself or me
80   In personal action, yet prodigious grown
    And fearful, as these strange eruptions are.

CASCA: Whoever knew the heavens to be this upset?

CASSIUS: Those who have known the earth to be full of faults. For my part, I have walked about the streets during this perilous night and, Casca, as you see, with my coat open and my bosom naked to the thunderstorm; and when the cross blue lightning seemed to open the breast of heaven, I did expose myself to its aim and very flash.

CASCA: But why do you tempt the heavens? It is the part of men to fear and tremble when the most mighty gods send such dreadful heralds to astonish us.

CASSIUS: You are dull, Casca, and you lack those sparks of life that should be in a Roman, or else you don't use them. You look pale, gaze amazedly, and put on fear and wonder when you see the strange occurrences of the heavens. If you would only consider the true cause of why these fires, gliding ghosts, strange birds, and beasts abound; why old men trick, and children predict the future; and why all these things change from their natural order into monstrous qualities—why, you will then find that heaven has infused them with these spirits to make them instruments of fear and warning of the current monstrous state. I could now, Casca, name a man most like this dreadful night, who thunders, lightnings, opens graves, and roars as the lion in the Capitol does. He is a man no mightier than yourself or me in personal action, yet he has grown as great and fearful as these strange eruptions.

CASCA: 'Tis Caesar that you mean, is it not, Cassius?

CASSIUS: Let it be who it is, for Romans now
    Have thews and limbs like to their ancestors.
85   But, woe the while! Our fathers' minds are dead,
    And we are govern'd with our mothers' spirits;
    Our yoke and sufferance show us womanish.

CASCA: Indeed they say the senators tomorrow
    Mean to establish Caesar as a king,
90   And he shall wear his crown by sea and land,
    In every place save here in Italy.

CASSIUS: I know where I will wear this dagger then:
    Cassius from bondage will deliver Cassius.
    Therein, ye gods, you make the weak most strong;
95   Therein, ye gods, you tyrants do defeat.
    Nor stony tower, nor walls of beaten brass,
    Nor airless dungeon, nor strong links of iron,
    Can be retentive to the strength of spirit;
    But life, being weary of these worldly bars,
100   Never lacks power to dismiss itself.
    If I know this, know all the world besides,
    That part of tyranny that I do bear
    I can shake off at pleasure.   *[Thunder still.]*

CASCA: So can I.
105   So every bondman in his own hand bears
    The power to cancel his captivity.

CASSIUS: And why should Caesar be a tyrant then?
    Poor man! I know he would not be a wolf
    But that he sees the Romans are but sheep.
110   He were no lion, were not Romans hinds.
    Those that with haste will make a mighty fire
    Begin it with weak straws. What trash is Rome,
    What rubbish and what offal, when it serves
    For the base matter to illuminate

CASCA: *It is Caesar that you mean, is it not, Cassius?*

CASSIUS: *Let it be who it is. Romans still have sinews and limbs like their ancestors did. But, woe the day! Our fathers' minds are dead, and we are governed with our mothers' weaker spirits; our yoke and suffering show us to be womanish.*

CASCA: *Indeed they say the senators mean to establish Caesar as a king tomorrow. He will wear his crown everywhere except here in Italy.*

CASSIUS: *I know where I will wear this dagger then; Cassius from slavery will deliver Cassius. Therein, you gods, you make the weak most strong; therein, you gods do defeat tyrants. No stone towers, nor walls of beaten brass, no airless dungeon, nor strong links of iron can restrain the strength of spirit. A life, being weary of these worldly bars, never lacks the power to end its own life. If I know this then, know all the world besides that part of tyranny that I do bear, I can shake it off at my own pleasure.* [Thunder still.]

CASCA: *So can I. So every slave bears the power to cancel his own captivity with his own hand.*

CASSIUS: *And why should Caesar be a tyrant then? Poor man! I know he would not be a wolf except that he sees the Romans are but sheep. He were no lion were not the Romans deer. Those who would make a mighty fire in haste begin it with only weak straws. What trash is Rome! What rubbish, and what chips, when it serves for the base matter to illuminate so worthless a thing as Caesar? But, grief, where have you led me? I perhaps speak this before a willing slave; then I know my answer must be made. But I am armed, and dangers are not intimidating to me.*

115   So vile a thing as Caesar? But, O grief,
         Where hast thou led me? I perhaps speak this
         Before a willing bondman; then I know
         My answer must be made. But I am arm'd,
         And dangers are to me indifferent.

120   CASCA: You speak to Casca, and to such a man
         That is no fleering tell-tale. Hold, my hand.
         Be factious for redress of all these griefs,
         And I will set this foot of mine as far
         As who goes farthest.

125   CASSIUS: There's a bargain made.
         Now know you, Casca, I have moved already
         Some certain of the noblest-minded Romans
         To undergo with me an enterprise
         Of honorable-dangerous consequence;
130   And I do know, by this they stay for me
         In Pompey's Porch. For now, this fearful night,
         There is no stir or walking in the streets,
         And the complexion of the element
         In favor's like the work we have in hand,
135   Most bloody, fiery, and most terrible.

[Enter Cinna.]

CASCA: Stand close awhile, for here comes one in haste.

CASSIUS: 'Tis Cinna, I do know him by his gait;
         He is a friend. Cinna, where haste you so?

CINNA: To find out you. Who's that? Metellus Cimber?

140   CASSIUS: No, it is Casca, one incorporate
         To our attempts. Am I not stay'd for, Cinna?

CINNA: I am glad on't. What a fearful night is this!
         There's two or three of us have seen strange sights.

CASCA: *You speak to Casca, and I am a man who is no mocking tattletale. Hold my hand. Form a faction for redress of all these griefs, and I will set this foot of mine as far as any who goes the farthest.*

CASSIUS: *Here's a bargain made. [Shakes hands.] Now you know, Casca, I have already moved some of the noblest-minded Romans to undergo with me an enterprise of honorable but dangerous consequence. And I do know that they wait for me at Pompey's theatre. For now, during this fearful night, there are none stirring or walking in the streets. The complexion of the night is most like the work we have in hand—most bloody, most fiery, and most terrible.*

[Enter Cinna.]

CASCA: *Keep concealed, for here someone comes in haste.*

CASSIUS: *It is Cinna. I do know him by his walk; he is a friend. Cinna, where are you going so quickly?*

CINNA: *To find you. Who's that? Metellus Cimber?*

CASSIUS: *No, it is Casca—one who is party to our attempts. Am I not waited for, Cinna?*

CINNA: *I am glad of it. What a fearful night this is! There are two or three of us who have seen strange sights.*

CASSIUS: Am I not stay'd for? Tell me.

145 CINNA: Yes, you are.
    O Cassius, if you could
    But win the noble Brutus to our party—

CASSIUS: Be you content. Good Cinna, take this paper,
    And look you lay it in the praetor's chair,
150   Where Brutus may but find it; and throw this
    In at his window; set this up with wax
    Upon old Brutus' statue. All this done,
    Repair to Pompey's porch, where you shall find us.
    Is Decius Brutus and Trebonius there?

155 CINNA: All but Metellus Cimber, and he's gone
    To seek you at your house. Well, I will hie
    And so bestow these papers as you bade me.

CASSIUS: That done, repair to Pompey's theatre.
                       [Exit Cinna.]
    Come, Casca, you and I will yet ere day
160   See Brutus at his house. Three parts of him
    Is ours already, and the man entire
    Upon the next encounter yields him ours.

CASCA: O, he sits high in all the people's hearts,
    And that which would appear offense in us,
165   His countenance, like richest alchemy,
    Will change to virtue and to worthiness.

CASSIUS: Him and his worth and our great need of him
    You have right well conceited. Let us go,
    For it is after midnight, and ere day
175   We will awake him and be sure of him.   *[Exeunt.]*

CASSIUS: *Am I not waited for? Tell me.*

CINNA: *Yes, you are. Oh, Cassius, if you could only win the noble Brutus to our party—*

CASSIUS: *Be content. Good Cinna, take this paper and lay it on the judge's chair where Brutus will find it. And throw this into his window; set this up with wax upon old Brutus' statue. When all this is done, come to Pompey's theatre where you shall find us. Are Decius Brutus and Trebonius there?*

CINNA: *All but Metellus Cimber—and he's gone to seek you at your house. Well, I will go and distribute these papers as you asked me.*

CASSIUS: *That being finished, come to Pompey's theatre.*
[Exit Cinna.]
Come, Casca, you and I need to go today to see Brutus at his house. Three parts of him are ours already, and the entire man yields to us at our next meeting.

CASCA: *Oh, he sits high in all the people's hearts. That which would appear offensive in us, Brutus' face will change to virtue and to worthiness.*

CASSIUS: *You are right that we need him very much. Let us go, for it is after midnight. Before daybreak we will awaken him and be certain of his loyalty.* [Exit.]

ACT II

SCENE 1

[Enter Brutus in his orchard.]

BRUTUS: What, Lucius, ho!
    I cannot, by the progress of the stars,
    Gives guess how near to day. Lucius, I say!
    I would it were my fault to sleep so soundly.
5   When, Lucius, when? awake, I say! what, Lucius!

[Enter Lucius.]

LUCIUS: Call'd you, my lord?

BRUTUS: Get me a taper in my study, Lucius.
    When it is lighted, come and call me here.

LUCIUS: I will, my lord.   *[Exit.]*

10 BRUTUS: It must be by his death, and, for my part,
    I know no personal cause to spurn at him,
    But for the general. He would be crown'd:
    How that might change his nature, there's the question.
    It is the bright day that brings forth the adder
15   And that craves wary walking. Crown him?—that;—
    And then, I grant, we put a sting in him
    That at his will he may do danger with.
    The abuse of greatness is when it disjoins

ACT II

SCENE 1

[Enter Brutus in his orchard.]

BRUTUS: *What, Lucius, hello! I cannot, by the lack of stars, guess how near it is to daybreak. Lucius, I say! I wish that I could sleep so soundly. Well, Lucius, hello? Awake, I say! Hey, Lucius!*

[Enter Lucius.]

LUCIUS: *Did you call, my lord?*

BRUTUS: *Get me a candle in my study, Lucius. When it is lit, come and call me.*

LUCIUS: *I will, my lord.*   [Exit.]

BRUTUS: *It must be by his death and for my part, I know no personal cause to spurn at him except those of a general nature. He might be crowned. How that might change his nature — there's the question. It is the brightest day that brings forth the snakes which cause wary walking. Crown him? If we do, I grant we will put a sting in him that, at his will, he may do dangerous things with. The abuse of greatness is when it disconnects compassion from power. To speak true of Caesar, I have not known when his passions controlled more than his reason. But it is a common proof that such beginnings are young ambition's ladder to which the climber*

Remorse from power, and, to speak truth of Caesar,
20   I have not known when his affections sway'd
More than his reason. But 'tis a common proof
That lowliness is young ambition's ladder,
Whereto the climber-upward turns his face;
But when he once attains the upmost round,
25   He then unto the ladder turns his back,
Looks in the clouds, scorning the base degrees
By which he did ascend. So Caesar may;
Then, lest he may, prevent. And, since the quarrel
Will bear no color for the thing he is,
30   Fashion it thus, that what he is, augmented,
Would run to these and these extremities;
And therefore think him as a serpent's egg
Which hatch'd would as his kind grow mischievous,
And kill him in the shell.

[Re-enter Lucius.]

35   LUCIUS: The taper burneth in your closet, sir.
Searching the window for a flint I found
This paper thus seal'd up, and I am sure
It did not lie there when I went to bed.

[Gives him the letter.]

BRUTUS: Get you to bed again, it is not day.
40   Is not tomorrow, boy, the ides of March?

LUCIUS: I know not, sir.

BRUTUS: Look in the calendar and bring me word.

LUCIUS: I will, sir.   *[Exit.]*

BRUTUS: The exhalations whizzing in the air
45   Give so much light that I may read by them.
[Opens the letter and reads.]

turns his face upward. Once he attains the utmost rung, he then turns his back on the ladder—looking at the clouds and scorning the poor fellows who helped him ascend. So Caesar may. Then, since he might, we must prevent it. And, since the quarrel will bear no connection to the man we know, we must fashion it thus. What he is will be changed into something extreme. Therefore, think of him as a serpent's egg which, when hatched, would grow dangerous and kill him in the shell.

[Re-enter Lucius.]

LUCIUS: *The candle burns in your room, sir. Searching the window for a flint, I found this sealed paper, which, I am sure, was not lying there when I went to bed.*　　　　　　　　　　[Gives him the letter.]

BRUTUS: *Get to bed again; it is not yet day. Is not tomorrow, boy, the fifteenth of March?*

LUCIUS: *I do not know, sir.*

BRUTUS: *Look in the calendar and bring me word.*

LUCIUS: *I will, sir.*　　　　　　　　　　　　[Exit.]

BRUTUS: *The comets whizzing in the air give so much light that I may read by them.*
　　　　　　　　[Opens the letter and reads.]

"Brutus, thou sleep'st: awake and see thyself!
Shall Rome, &c. Speak, strike, redress!"
"Brutus, thou sleep'st: awake!"

50 Such instigations have been often dropp'd
Where I have took them up.
"Shall Rome, &c." Thus must I piece it out.
Shall Rome stand under one man's awe? What, Rome?
My ancestors did from the streets of Rome
55 The Tarquin drive, when he was call'd a king.
"Speak, strike, redress!" Am I entreated
To speak and strike? O Rome, I make thee promise,
If the redress will follow, thou receivest
Thy full petition at the hand of Brutus!

[Re-enter Lucius.]

60 LUCIUS: Sir, March is wasted fifteen days.
           [Knocking within.]

BRUTUS: 'Tis good. Go to the gate, somebody knocks.
           [Exit Lucius.]
Since Cassius first did whet me against Caesar
I have not slept.
Between the acting of a dreadful thing
65 And the first motion, all the interim is
Like a phantasma or a hideous dream;
The genius and the mortal instruments
Are then in council, and the state of man,
Like to a little kingdom, suffers then
70 The nature of an insurrection.

[Re-enter Lucius.]

LUCIUS: Sir, 'tis your brother Cassius at the door,
 Who doth desire to see you.

BRUTUS: Is he alone?

"Brutus, you sleep. Awake and see yourself!
Shall Rome, etc. Speak, strike, redress!"
"Brutus, you sleep. Awake!"

Such instigations have been often dropped where I have taken them up.
"Shall Rome, etc." Thus must I figure it out. Shall Rome stand under one
man's awe? What, Rome? My ancestors did from the streets of Rome
drive Tarquin when he was called a king. "Speak, strike, redress!" Am I
asked to speak and strike? Oh, Rome, I make you a promise. If the
redress is needed, you will receive your full petition at the hands of
Brutus!

[Re-enter Lucius.]

LUCIUS: *Sir, March has wasted fifteen days.*

[Knocking within.]

BRUTUS: *It is good. Go to the gate; somebody knocks.*

[Exit Lucius.]

Since Cassius first warned me of Caesar, I have not slept. Between the
acting of a dreadful thing and the first motion, all the time between is
like a hallucination or a hideous nightmare. The soul and my thoughts
are then in council. The state of man, like a little kingdom, suffers, there-
fore, the nature of a war.

[Re-enter Lucius.]

LUCIUS: *Sir, it is your brother, Cassius, at the door. He desires to see you.*

BRUTUS: *Is he alone?*

51

LUCIUS: No, sir, there are moe with him.

75   BRUTUS: Do you know them?

LUCIUS: No, sir, their hats are pluck'd about their ears,
   And half their faces buried in their cloaks,
   That by no means I may discover them
   By any mark of favor.

80   BRUTUS: Let 'em enter.   *[Exit Lucius.]*
   They are the faction. O Conspiracy,
   Shamest thou to show thy dangerous brow by night,
   When evils are most free? O, then, by day
   Where wilt thou find a cavern dark enough
85   To mask thy monstrous visage? Seek none, conspiracy;
   Hide it in smiles and affability;
   For if thou path, thy native semblance on,
   Not Erebus itself were dim enough
   To hide thee from prevention.

[Enter the conspirators, Cassius, Casca, Decius, Cinna, Metellus Cimber, and Trebonius.]

90   CASSIUS: I think we are too bold upon your rest.
   Good morrow, Brutus, do we trouble you?

BRUTUS: I have been up this hour, awake all night.
   Know I these men that come along with you?

CASSIUS: Yes, every man of them, and no man here
95   But honors you, and every one doth wish
   You had but that opinion of yourself
   Which every noble Roman bears of you.
   This is Trebonius.

BRUTUS: He is welcome hither.

100   CASSIUS: This, Decius Brutus.

52

LUCIUS: *No, sir. There are more with him.*

BRUTUS: *Do you know them?*

LUCIUS: *No, sir. Their hats are drawn around their ears, and half their faces are buried in their cloaks so that by no means may I discern who they are.*

BRUTUS: *Let them enter.*   [Exit Lucius.]
    They are the faction. Conspiracy, do you feel shame to show your dangerous face by night when evils are the most free? Where will you find a cave dark enough to hide your monstrous face during the day? Seek none; conspiracy hides itself in smiles and affability. If you take this path which appears now, not even hell itself were dark enough to hide you.

[Enter the conspirators: Cassius, Casca, Decius, Cinna, Metellus Cimber, and Trebonius.]

CASSIUS: *I think we have disturbed your rest. Good morning, Brutus. Do we trouble you?*

BRUTUS: *I have been up this hour and awake all night. Do I know these men that accompany you?*

CASSIUS: *Yes, every one of them. Every man here honors you, and everyone does wish you had that opinion of yourself which every noble Roman bears of you. This is Trebonius.*

BRUTUS: *He is welcome here.*

CASSIUS: *This, Decius Brutus.*

BRUTUS: He is welcome too.

CASSIUS: This, Casca; this, Cinna; and this, Metellus Cimber.

BRUTUS: They are all welcome.
    What watchful cares do interpose themselves
105   Betwixt your eyes and night?

CASSIUS: Shall I entreat a word?   *[They whisper.]*

DECIUS: Here lies the east. Doth not the day break here?

CASCA: No.

CINNA: O, pardon, sir, it doth, and yon grey lines
110   That fret the clouds are messengers of day.

CASCA: You shall confess that you are both deceived.
    Here, as I point my sword, the sun arises,
    Which is a great way growing on the south,
    Weighing the youthful season of the year.
115   Some two months hence up higher toward the north
    He first presents his fire, and the high east
    Stands as the Capitol, directly here.

BRUTUS: Give me your hands all over, one by one.

CASSIUS: And let us swear our resolution.

120 BRUTUS: No, not an oath. If not the face of men,
    The sufferance of our souls, the time's abuse—
    If these be motives weak, break off betimes,
    And every man hence to his idle bed;
    So let high-sighted tyranny range on
125   Till each man drop by lottery. But if these,
    As I am sure they do, bear fire enough
    To kindle cowards and to steel with valor

54

BRUTUS: He is welcome, too.

CASSIUS: This, Casca; this, Cinna; and this, Metellus Cimber.

BRUTUS: They are all welcome. What cares come between your eyes and sleep tonight?

CASSIUS: May I entreat a word with you? [Brutus and Cassius step to side and speak in hushed voices.]

DECIUS: Here lies the east. Does not the day break here?

CASCA: No.

CINNA: Oh, pardon, sir, it does; the gray lines on the horizon which fret the clouds are messengers of day.

CASCA: You will confess that you are both deceived. Here, as I point my sword, is where the sun rises, growing on the south this time of year. Some two months from now it will be higher toward the north where it first presents its fire. The high east stands as the Capitol, directly here.

[Brutus and Cassius return.]

BRUTUS: Give me your hands all over again, one by one.

CASSIUS: And let us swear our resolution.

BRUTUS: No, not an oath. If the faces of men do not reflect the suffering of our souls and the times abuses, then we have only weak motives and should leave these thoughts and go instead to our beds; let tyranny live while we are dropped by chance one by one. But if these facts, as I am sure they do, bear fire enough to kindle cowards and to strengthen the melting spirits of women, then, countrymen, we do not need anything but our own cause to move us to action. As Romans, we do not need anything more than our promises to insure their action. Other than our honor,

The melting spirits of women, then, countrymen,
What need we any spur but our own cause
130 To prick us to redress? What other bond
Than secret Romans that have spoke the word
And will not palter? And what other oath
Than honesty to honesty engaged
That this shall be or we will fall for it?
135 Swear priests and cowards and men cautelous,
Old feeble carrions and such suffering souls
That welcome wrongs; unto bad causes swear
Such creatures as men doubt; but do not stain
The even virtue of our enterprise,
140 Nor the insuppressive mettle of our spirits,
To think that or our cause or our performance
Did need an oath; when every drop of blood
That every Roman bears, and nobly bears,
Is guilty of a several bastardy
145 If he do break the smallest particle
Of any promise that hath pass'd from him.

CASSIUS: But what of Cicero? Shall we sound him?
I think he will stand very strong with us.

CASCA: Let us not leave him out.

150 CINNA: No, by no means.

METELLUS: O, let us have him, for his silver hairs
Will purchase us a good opinion,
And buy men's voices to commend our deeds.
It shall be said his judgement ruled our hands;
155 Our youths and wildness shall no whit appear,
But all be buried in his gravity.

BRUTUS: O, name him not; let us not break with him,
For he will never follow anything
That other men begin.

what oath will engage us? Let oaths be sworn by priests and cowards as well as by deceitful, elderly, dying men and such suffering souls who welcome lies. But do not stain the virtue of our enterprise or the courage of our spirits to think that our cause or our performance needs an oath. Every drop of Roman blood nobly borne is guilty of a severe sin if he breaks even the smallest particle of any promise that he has given.

CASSIUS: *But what of Cicero? Should we sound him out about this matter? I think he will stand strongly with us.*

CASCA: *Let us not leave him out.*

CINNA: *No, by no means.*

METELLUS: *Let us have him; for his advanced age will gain us good opinion and buy men's voices to commend our deeds. It will be said that his judgment ruled our hands, that our youth and boldness will not appear but rather be buried in his grave tones.*

BRUTUS: *Forget about him; let us not talk to him. He will never follow anything that other men begin.*

160 CASSIUS: Then leave him out.

CASCA: Indeed he is not fit.

DECIUS: Shall no man else be touch'd but only Caesar?

CASSIUS: Decius, well urged. I think it is not meet
      Mark Antony, so well beloved of Caesar,
165   Should outlive Caesar. We shall find of him
      A shrewd contriver; and you know his means,
      If he improve them, may well stretch so far
      As to annoy us all, which to prevent,
      Let Antony and Caesar fall together.

175 BRUTUS: Our course will seem too bloody, Caius Cassius,
      To cut the head off and then hack the limbs
      Like wrath in death and envy afterwards;
      For Antony is but a limb of Caesar.
      Let us be sacrificers, but not butchers, Caius.
180   We all stand up against the spirit of Caesar,
      And in the spirit of men there is no blood.
      O, that we then could come by Caesar's spirit,
      And not dismember Caesar! But, alas,
      Caesar must bleed for it! And, gentle friends,
185   Let's kill him boldly, but not wrathfully;
      Let's carve him as a dish fit for the gods,
      Not hew him as a carcass fit for hounds;
      And let our hearts, as subtle masters do,
      Stir up their servants to an act of rage
190   And after seem to chide 'em. This shall make
      Our purpose necessary and not envious,
      Which so appearing to the common eyes,
      We shall be call'd purgers, not murderers.
      And for Mark Antony, think not of him,
195   For he can do no more than Caesar's arm
      When Caesar's head is off.

CASSIUS: *Then leave him out.*

CASCA: *Indeed he is not fit.*

DECIUS: *Will anyone else be killed but Caesar?*

CASSIUS: *Well said, Decius. I do not think it is not right that Mark Antony, so well beloved of Caesar, should outlive him. We shall find in him a shrewd foe. And you know that with his resources—if he improves them—he may well become a problem to us all. To prevent this, let Antony and Caesar fall together.*

BRUTUS: *Our course will seem too bloody, Caius Cassius; to cut the head off and then hack the limbs, too—it is like revenge in death and hatred afterwards. Antony is only a limb of Caesar. Let us be scarifiers, but not butchers, Caius. We will all stand up against the spirit of Caesar, and in the spirit of men there needs to be shed no blood. Oh, that we then could come by Caesar's soul, and yet not dismember Caesar! But, alas, Caesar must bleed for it! And, good friends, let's kill him boldly, not hatefully; let's carve him as a dish fit for the gods, not hew him as a carcass fit for dogs. Let our hearts, as subtle masters do, stir our hands to this murder but scold them after the deed is done. This shall make our purpose seem necessary and not a cause done because of envy. When this appears so to the common eyes, we shall be called cleansers, not murderers. As for Mark Antony, think not of him. He can do no more than Caesar's arm could do when Caesar's head is off.*

CASSIUS: Yet I fear him,
  For in the ingrated love he bears to Caesar—

BRUTUS: Alas, good Cassius, do not think of him.
200   If he love Caesar, all that he can do
  Is to himself, take thought and die for Caesar.
  And that were much he should, for he is given
  To sports, to wildness, and much company.

TREBONIUS: There is no fear in him, let him not die,
205   For he will live and laugh at this hereafter.   *[Clock strikes.]*

BRUTUS: Peace, count the clock.

CASSIUS: The clock hath stricken three.

TREBONIUS: 'Tis time to part.

CASSIUS: But it is doubtful yet
210   Whether Caesar will come forth today or no,
  For he is superstitious grown of late,
  Quite from the main opinion he held once
  Of fantasy, of dreams and ceremonies.
  It may be these apparent prodigies,
215   The unaccustom'd terror of this night,
  And the persuasion of his augurers
  May hold him from the Capitol today.

DECIUS: Never fear that. If he be so resolved,
  I can o'ersway him, for he loves to hear
220   That unicorns may be betray'd with trees,
  And bears with glasses, elephants with holes,
  Lions with toils, and men with flatterers;
  But when I tell him he hates flatterers,
  He says he does, being then most flattered.
225   Let me work;
  For I can give his humor the true bent,
  And I will bring him to the Capitol.

CASSIUS: *Yet I fear him because of the ingrained love he bears for Caesar—*

BRUTUS: *Alas, good Cassius, do not think of him. If he loves Caesar, the only thing he can do is to kill himself: think and kill himself for Caesar. But that is very unlikely, since he likes sports, wildness, and much socializing.*

TREBONIUS: *There is nothing to fear in him—let him not die; for he will live and laugh at this hereafter.* [Clock strikes.]

BRUTUS: *Peace! Count the clock strikes.*

CASSIUS: *The clock has struck three.*

TREBONIUS: *It is time to part.*

CASSIUS: *But it is still doubtful whether Caesar will come to the Senate today. He has grown superstitious lately, quite contrary to the main opinion he once held of fantasy, dreams, and rites. It may be that these apparent changes and the unusual terrors of this night and the persuasion of his fortune-tellers may keep him from the Capitol today.*

DECIUS: *Never fear that. If he is so resolved, I can sway him. He loves to hear that unicorns may be trapped with trees and bears with mirrors, elephants with holes, lions with nets, and men with flatterers. When I tell him he hates flatterers, he says he does and is thus most flattered. Let me do my work; for I can manipulate him without his knowing it, and I will bring him to the Capitol.*

CASSIUS: Nay, we will all of us be there to fetch him.

BRUTUS: By the eighth hour. Is that the uttermost?

230 CINNA: Be that the uttermost, and fail not then.

METELLUS: Caius Ligarius doth bear Caesar hard,
    Who rated him for speaking well of Pompey.
    I wonder none of you have thought of him.

BRUTUS: Now, good Metellus, go along by him.
235   He loves me well, and I have given him reasons;
    Send him but hither, and I'll fashion him.

CASSIUS: The morning comes upon's. We'll leave you, Brutus,
    And, friends, disperse yourselves, but all remember
    What you have said and show yourselves true Romans.

240 BRUTUS: Good gentlemen, look fresh and merrily;
    Let not our looks put on our purposes,
    But bear it as our Roman actors do,
    With untired spirits and formal constancy.
    And so, good morrow to you every one.
                     [Exeunt all but Brutus.]
245   Boy! Lucius! Fast asleep? It is no matter.
    Enjoy the honey-heavy dew of slumber;
    Thou hast no figures nor no fantasies,
    Which busy care draws in the brains of men;
    Therefore thou sleep'st so sound.

[Enter Portia.]

250 PORTIA: Brutus, my lord!

BRUTUS: Portia, what mean you? Wherefore rise you now?
    It is not for your health thus to commit
    Your weak condition to the raw cold morning.

CASSIUS: No. We all will be there to fetch him.

BRUTUS: By eight o'clock at the latest?

CINNA: No later, and do not fail.

METELLUS: Caius Ligarius bears Caesar a grudge since he berated him for speaking well of Pompey. I wonder that none of you have thought of him.

BRUTUS: Now, good Metellus, go to him. He loves me highly, and I have given him reasons. Send him here, and I'll turn him.

CASSIUS: The morning comes upon us. We'll leave you, Brutus. Friends, disperse yourselves; but all remember what you have said and show yourselves to be true Romans.

BRUTUS: Good gentlemen, look fresh and merry; do not let our looks show our purposes, but bear it as our Roman actors do with untried spirits and firmness of mind. And so, good morning to you all.
                                        [Exit all but Brutus.]
Boy! Lucius! Fast asleep? It is no matter. Enjoy the honey-heavy dew of slumber. You have no imaginings and no fantasies which busy care draws into the brains of men. Therefore, you sleep so soundly.

[Enter Portia.]

PORTIA: Brutus, my lord!

BRUTUS: Portia, what does all this mean? Why do you rise now? It is not good for your health to thus commit your weak condition to the raw cold morning.

PORTIA: Nor for yours neither. have ungently, Brutus,
255   Stole from my bed; and yesternight at supper
You suddenly arose and walk'd about,
Musing and sighing, with your arms across;
And when I ask'd you what the matter was,
You stared upon me with ungentle looks.
260   I urged you further; then you scratch'd your head,
And too impatiently stamp'd with your foot.
Yet I insisted, yet you answer'd not,
But with an angry wafture of your hand
Gave sign for me to leave you. So I did,
265   Fearing to strengthen that impatience
Which seem'd too much enkindled, and withal
Hoping it was but an effect of humor,
Which sometime hath his hour with every man.
It will not let you eat, nor talk, nor sleep,
270   And, could it work so much upon your shape
As it hath much prevail'd on your condition,
I should not know you, Brutus. Dear my lord,
Make me acquainted with your cause of grief.

BRUTUS: I am not well in health, and that is all.

275 PORTIA: Brutus is wise, and, were he not in health,
He would embrace the means to come by it.

BRUTUS: Why, so I do. Good Portia, go to bed.

PORTIA: Is Brutus sick, and is it physical
To walk unbraced and suck up the humors
280   Of the dank morning? What, is Brutus sick,
And will he steal out of his wholesome bed
To dare the vile contagion of the night
And tempt the rheumy and unpurged air
To add unto his sickness? No, my Brutus,
285   You have some sick offense within your mind,
Which by the right and virtue of my place
I ought to know of; and, upon my knees,

PORTIA: *Nor for yours, either. You are not courteous, lord, in stealing from my bed. Further, last night at supper you suddenly rose and walked about, contemplating and sighing with your arms crossed. When I asked you what was the matter, you stared at me with rugged looks. I watched you further and you scratched your head and impatiently stamped your foot. When I insisted, you would not answer. Instead, with an angry waving of your hand, you gave me a sign to leave you. I did so, fearing to strengthen your impatience, which seemed too much fired. I was hoping it was only an effect of one of your humors which sometime has his way with every man. It will not let you eat, nor talk, nor sleep. If it could work so much upon your shape as it has prevailed upon your mind, I should not know you, Brutus. Dear, my lord, acquaint me with your cause of grief.*

BRUTUS: *I am not well in health, and that is all.*

PORTIA: *Brutus is wise; and, if he were not in health, he would find a way to cure his illness.*

BRUTUS: *Why, so I do. Good Portia, go to bed.*

PORTIA: *Is Brutus sick? Is it healthy to walk without proper clothes and suck up the humors of this damp morning? What, is Brutus sick? Will he steal out of his wholesome bed to dare the vile sickness of the night and tempt the damp and unclean air to further his sickness? No, my Brutus; you have some sick offense within your mind which by the right and virtue of my marriage I ought to know. Upon my knees I beg you, by my once commended beauty, and by all your vows of love and that great wedding vow which did connect and make us one, that you tell to me, your other half, why you are so grave. Further, tell me why men tonight*

I charm you, by my once commended beauty,
By all your vows of love and that great vow
290 Which did incorporate and make us one,
That you unfold to me, yourself, your half,
Why you are heavy, and what men tonight
Have had resort to you; for here have been
Some six or seven, who did hide their faces
295 Even from darkness.

BRUTUS: Kneel not, gentle Portia.

PORTIA: I should not need, if you were gentle Brutus.
Within the bond of marriage, tell me, Brutus,
Is it excepted I should know no secrets
300 That appertain to you? Am I yourself
But, as it were, in sort or limitation,
To keep with you at meals, comfort your bed,
And talk to you sometimes? Dwell I but in the suburbs
Of your good pleasure? If it be no more,
305 Portia is Brutus' harlot, not his wife.

BRUTUS: You are my true and honorable wife,
As dear to me as are the ruddy drops
That visit my sad heart.

PORTIA: If this were true, then should I know this secret.
310 I grant I am a woman, but withal
A woman that Lord Brutus took to wife.
I grant I am a woman, but withal
A woman well reputed, Cato's daughter.
Think you I am no stronger than my sex,
315 Being so father'd and so husbanded?
Tell me your counsels, I will not disclose em.
I have made strong proof of my constancy,
Giving myself a voluntary wound
Here in the thigh. Can I bear that with patience
320 And not my husband's secrets?

have come to you; for there have been some six or seven who hid their faces even from the darkness.

[Prepares to beg him on her knees for an answer.]

BRUTUS: Do not kneel, sweet Portia.

PORTIA: I should not need to if you were sweet Brutus. By our bond of marriage, tell me, Brutus. Should I know no secrets which pertain to you? Am I only here in a limited way to keep you company at meals, comfort your bed, and talk to you sometimes? Do I dwell only in the outskirts of your good pleasure? If it is only this, Portia is Brutus' harlot, not his wife.

BRUTUS: You are my true and honorable wife—as dear to me as are the bloody drops that visit my sad heart.

PORTIA: If this were true, then I should know this secret. I grant you, I am merely a woman but most certainly the woman that Lord Brutus took as his wife. I grant you I am only a woman, but most certainly a woman with a good reputation—Cato's daughter. Do you think I am no stronger than my sex, having such a strong background? Tell me your counsels, I will not disclose them. [Thrusts a knife into her thigh.] I have proven my loyalty, giving myself a voluntary wound here in the thigh. Can I bear that with patience and not my husband's secrets?

BRUTUS: O ye gods,
    Render me worthy of this noble wife!   *[Knocking within.]*
    Hark, hark, one knocks. Portia, go in awhile,
    And by and by thy bosom shall partake
325   The secrets of my heart.
    All my engagements I will construe to thee,
    All the charactery of my sad brows.
    Leave me with haste. *[Exit Portia.]* Lucius, who's that knocks?

[Re-enter Lucius with Ligarius.]

LUCIUS: Here is a sick man that would speak with you.

330 BRUTUS: Caius Ligarius, that Metellus spake of.
    Boy, stand aside. Caius Ligarius, how?

LIGARIUS: Vouchsafe good morrow from a feeble tongue.

BRUTUS: O, what a time have you chose out, brave Caius,
335   To wear a kerchief! Would you were not sick!

LIGARIUS: I am not sick, if Brutus have in hand
    Any exploit worthy the name of honor.

BRUTUS: Such an exploit have I in hand, Ligarius,
    Had you a healthful ear to hear of it.

340 LIGARIUS: By all the gods that Romans bow before,
    I here discard my sickness! Soul of Rome!
    Brave son, derived from honorable loins!
    Thou, like an exorcist, hast conjured up
    My mortified spirit. Now bid me run,
345   And I will strive with things impossible,
    Yea, get the better of them. What's to do?

BRUTUS: A piece of work that will make sick men whole.

LIGARIUS: But are not some whole that we must make sick?

BRUTUS: *You gods, prove me worthy to have this noble wife!*

[Knocking within]

Hark, hark! Someone knocks. Portia, go in awhile. Soon you shall share the secrets of my heart. All my engagements I will tell to you; all the reasons for my sad brows. Leave me with haste. [Exit Portia.] *Lucius, who is it who knocks?*

[Re-enter Lucius with Ligarius.]

LUCIUS: *It is a sick man who would speak with you.*

BRUTUS: *It must be Caius Ligarius, of whom Metellus spoke. Boy, stand aside. Caius Ligarius! How are you?*

LIGARIUS: *Please accept a morning greeting from my feeble tongue.*

BRUTUS: *What a time have you chosen, brave Caius, to be sickly! I wish you were not sick!*

LIGARIUS: *I am not sick if Brutus has any exploit worthy of the name of honor in his hands.*

BRUTUS: *Such an exploit I have, Ligarius, if you have a healthful ear to hear it.*

LIGARIUS: *By all the gods that Romans bow before, I here discard my illness! Soul of Rome! Brave son, derived from honorable ancestry! You are like an exorcist who has conjured up my dead spirit. Bid me run and I will strive to do impossible things; I'll get the better of them. What's to do?*

BRUTUS: *A piece of work that will make sick men whole.*

LIGARIUS: *But are not some whole whom we must make sick?*

69

BRUTUS: That must we also. What it is, my Caius,
350   I shall unfold to thee, as we are going
    To whom it must be done.

LIGARIUS: Set on your foot,
    And with a heart new-fired I follow you,
    To do I know not what; but it sufficeth
355   That Brutus leads me on.

BRUTUS: Follow me then.   *[Exeunt.]*

SCENE 2
Caesar's house. Thunder and lightning.

[Enter Caesar, in his night-gown.]

CAESAR: Nor heaven nor earth have been at peace tonight.
    Thrice hath Calpurnia in her sleep cried out,
    "Help, ho! They murder Caesar!" Who's within?

[Enter a Servant.]

SERVANT: My lord?

5   CAESAR: Go bid the priests do present sacrifice,
    And bring me their opinions of success.

SERVANT: I will, my lord.   *[Exit.]*

[Enter Calpurnia.]

CALPURNIA: What mean you, Caesar? Think you to walk forth?
    You shall not stir out of your house today.

BRUTUS: *That must we do also. What it is, my Caius, I will tell you as we walk toward him to whom it must be done.*

LIGARIUS: *Set on your path and with a new-fired heart, I will follow you to do that which I know not. It is sufficient to me that Brutus leads me on.*

BRUTUS: *Follow me then.*   [Exit.]

SCENE 2
Caesar's house. Thunder and lightning.

[Enter Caesar, in his nightgown.]

CAESAR: *Neither heaven nor earth has been at peace tonight. Three times Calpurnia cried out in her sleep, "Help, here! They murder Caesar!" Who's within?*

[Enter a Servant.]

SERVANT: *My lord?*

CAESAR: *Go bid the priests perform a sacrifice and bring me their opinions of our success.*

SERVANT: *I will, my lord.*   [Exit.]

[Enter Calpurnia.]

CALPURNIA: *What do you mean, Caesar? Are you going out today? Today, you should not stir out of your house.*

10 CAESAR: Caesar shall forth: the things that threaten'd me
   Ne'er look'd but on my back; when they shall see
   The face of Caesar, they are vanished.

   CALPURNIA: Caesar, I never stood on ceremonies,
   Yet now they fright me. There is one within,
15 Besides the things that we have heard and seen,
   Recounts most horrid sights seen by the watch.
   A lioness hath whelped in the streets;
   And graves have yawn'd, and yielded up their dead;
   Fierce fiery warriors fight upon the clouds,
20 In ranks and squadrons and right form of war,
   Which drizzled blood upon the Capitol;
   The noise of battle hurtled in the air,
   Horses did neigh and dying men did groan,
   And ghosts did shriek and squeal about the streets.
25 O Caesar! These things are beyond all use,
   And I do fear them.

   CAESAR: What can be avoided
   Whose end is purposed by the mighty gods?
   Yet Caesar shall go forth, for these predictions
30 Are to the world in general as to Caesar.

   CALPURNIA: When beggars die, there are no comets seen;
   The heavens themselves blaze forth the death of princes.

   CAESAR: Cowards die many times before their deaths;
   The valiant never taste of death but once.
35 Of all the wonders that I yet have heard,
   It seems to me most strange that men should fear
   Seeing that death, a necessary end,
   Will come when it will come.

   [Re-enter Servant.]
         What say the augurers?

CAESAR: *Caesar will go forth. Things which threaten me look only on my back. When I face them, they all vanish.*

CALPURNIA: *Caesar, I never believed in the omens, yet now they frighten me. Besides the things that we have heard and seen, there is someone within who recounts many horrid sights seen by the guards. A lioness has given birth in the streets, and graves have opened and yielded up their dead. In the clouds, fierce, fiery warriors fought in ranks and squadrons, and blood drizzled upon the Capitol. Noises of battle hurtled in the air, horses shrieked, dying men groaned, and ghosts squealed about the streets. Oh, Caesar! These things are beyond all use, and I do fear them.*

CAESAR: *What can be avoided when an end is fated by the mighty gods? Yet Caesar shall go forth. These predictions pertain in general to the world, not just to Caesar.*

CALPURNIA: *When beggars die, there are no comets seen. The heavens themselves blaze forth on the death of princes.*

CAESAR: *Cowards die many times before their deaths; the valiant taste death only once. Of all the wonders that I have heard, it seems to me most strange that men should fear death, a necessary end, which will come when it will come.*

[Re-enter Servant.]
   What do the fortune-tellers say?

40   SERVANT: They would not have you to stir forth today.
          Plucking the entrails of an offering forth,
          They could not find a heart within the beast.

      CAESAR: The gods do this in shame of cowardice.
45   Caesar should be a beast without a heart
          If he should stay at home today for fear.
          No, Caesar shall not. Danger knows full well
          That Caesar is more dangerous than he.
          We are two lions litter'd in one day,
50   And I the elder and more terrible.
          And Caesar shall go forth.

      CALPURNIA: Alas, my lord,
          Your wisdom is consumed in confidence.
          Do not go forth today. Call it my fear
55   That keeps you in the house and not your own.
          We'll send Mark Antony to the Senate-house,
          And he shall say you are not well today.
          Let me, upon my knee, prevail in this.

      CAESAR: Mark Antony shall say I am not well,
60   And, for thy humor, I will stay at home.

      [Enter Decius.]
          Here's Decius Brutus, he shall tell them so.

      DECIUS: Caesar, all hail! Good morrow, worthy Caesar!
          I come to fetch you to the Senate-house.

      CAESAR: And you are come in very happy time ,
65   To bear my greeting to the senators
          And tell them that I will not come today.
          Cannot, is false, and that I dare not, falser:
          I will not come today. Tell them so, Decius.

      CALPURNIA: Say he is sick.

SERVANT: *They would not have you leave your house. When they opened up the offering, they could not find a heart within the beast.*

CAESAR: *The gods do this to shame our cowardice. Caesar should be a beast without a heart if he should stay at home today in fear. No, Caesar shall not be a coward; danger knows full well that Caesar is more dangerous than he. We are like two lions born in one single day. I am the elder and more terrible—and Caesar will go forth.*

CALPURNIA: *Alas, my lord, your wisdom is consumed by your confidence. Do not go out today. You can say it is my fear that keeps you in the house and not your own. We'll send Mark Antony to the senate, and he shall say you are not well today.* [Kneeling.] *Let me, upon my knee, prevail in this.*

CAESAR: *Mark Antony shall say I am not well; and, for your humor, I will stay at home.*

[Enter Decius.]
Here's Decius Brutus; he shall tell them.

DECIUS: *Caesar, all hail! Good morning, worthy Caesar. I come to fetch you to the Senate.*

CAESAR: *You have come in a very happy time to bear my greetings to the senators and tell them that I will not come today. "Cannot" is false, and that I "dare not" falser yet. I "will not" come today. Tell them so, Decius.*

CALPURNIA: *Say he is sick.*

75

70   Caesar: Shall Caesar send a lie?
      Have I in conquest stretch'd mine arm so far
      To be afeard to tell greybeards the truth?
      Decius, go tell them Caesar will not come.

      Decius: Most mighty Caesar, let me know some cause,
75   Lest I be laugh'd at when I tell them so.

      Caesar: The cause is in my will: I will not come,
      That is enough to satisfy the Senate.
      But, for your private satisfaction,
      Because I love you, I will let you know.
80   Calpurnia here, my wife, stays me at home;
      She dreamt tonight she saw my statue,
      Which like a fountain with an hundred spouts,
      Did run pure blood, and many lusty Romans
      Came smiling and did bathe their hands in it.
85   And these does she apply for warnings and portents
      And evils imminent, and on her knee
      Hath begg'd that I will stay at home today.

      Decius: This dream is all amiss interpreted;
90   It was a vision fair and fortunate.
      Your statue spouting blood in many pipes,
      In which so many smiling Romans bathed,
      Signifies that from you great Rome shall suck
      Reviving blood, and that great men shall press
95   For tinctures, stains, relics, and cognizance.
      This by Calpurnia's dream is signified.

      Caesar: And this way have you well expounded it.

      Decius: I have, when you have heard what I can say.
      And know it now, the Senate have concluded
100   To give this day a crown to mighty Caesar.
      If you shall send them word you will not come,
      Their minds may change. Besides, it were a mock
      Apt to be render'd, for some one to say

CAESAR: Will Caesar send a lie? Have I stretched my arm so far in conquest to be afraid to tell old men the truth? Decius, go tell them Caesar will not come.

DECIUS: Most mighty Caesar. Let me know some reason so that I will not be laughed at when I tell them this.

CAESAR: The cause is in my will; I will not come. That is enough to satisfy the Senate. But for your personal knowledge, because I like you, I will let you know the truth. Calpurnia here, my wife, asks me to say at home. She dreamed tonight that she saw my statue run pure blood, like a fountain with a hundred spigots. Many lusty Romans came smiling and bathed their hands in it. These dreams she interprets as warnings and omens of future evil. Thus, on her knee, she has begged me to stay at home today.

DECIUS: This dream is wrongly interpreted; it was a vision both fair and fortunate. Your statue spouting blood in many pipes in which so many smiling Romans bathed signifies that from you great Rome shall suck reviving blood and that great men will press you for souvenirs, relics, and recognition. This is what Calpurnia's dream signified.

CAESAR: And you have explained it well.

DECIUS: I have news which needs your attention. The Senate has concluded this day to give Caesar a crown. If you send them word you will not come, their minds might change. Besides, some might be likely to tease you with comments like "Break up the Senate until some future time when Caesar's wife has better dreams." If Caesar hides himself, will they whisper, "Well, Caesar is afraid"? Pardon me, Caesar, but my great love for you bids me to be blunt.

77

"Break up the Senate till another time,
105   When Caesar's wife shall meet with better dreams."
If Caesar hide himself, shall they not whisper
"Lo, Caesar is afraid"?
Pardon me, Caesar, for my dear dear love
To your proceeding bids me tell you this,
110   And reason to my love is liable.

CAESAR: How foolish do your fears seem now, Calpurnia!
    I am ashamed I did yield to them.
    Give me my robe, for I will go.

[Enter Publius, Brutus, Ligarius, Metellus, Casca, Trebonius, and Cinna.]
    And look where Publius is come to fetch me.

115   PUBLIUS: Good morrow, Caesar.

CAESAR: Welcome, Publius.
    What, Brutus, are you stirr'd so early too?
    Good morrow, Casca. Caius Ligarius,
    Caesar was ne'er so much your enemy
120   As that same ague which hath made you lean.
    What is't o'clock?

BRUTUS: Caesar, 'tis strucken eight.

CAESAR: I thank you for your pains and courtesy.

[Enter Antony.]
    See, Antony, that revels long o' nights,
125   Is notwithstanding up. Good morrow, Antony.

ANTONY: So to most noble Caesar.

CAESAR: Bid them prepare within.
    I am to blame to be thus waited for.
    Now, Cinna; now, Metellus; what, Trebonius,

CAESAR: *How foolish your fears seem now, Calpurnia! I am ashamed that I yielded to them. Give me my robe, for I will go.*

[Enter Publius, Brutus, Ligarius, Metellus, Casca, Trebonius, and Cinna.]
   And look where Publius has come to fetch me.

PUBLIUS: *Good morning, Caesar.*

CAESAR: *Welcome, Publius. What, Brutus, have you stirred so early, too? Good morning, Casca. Caius Ligarius, Caesar was never as much your enemy as that illness which has made you lean. What is the time?*

BRUTUS: *Caesar, it has struck eight.*

CAESAR: *I thank you for your pains and courtesy.*

[Enter Antony.]
   See, even Antony is up after his long night of revels. Good morning, Antony.

ANTONY: *The same to you, Caesar.*

CAESAR: *Bid those within to prepare. I am to blame that we have waited this long. Well, Cinna; well, Metellus. And, Trebonius! I have an hour's talk in store for you. Remember that you call on me today. Be near to me that I may remember you.*

79

130   I have an hour's talk in store for you;
          Remember that you call on me today;
          Be near me, that I may remember you.

      TREBONIUS: Caesar, I will. *[Aside.]* And so near will I be
      That your best friends shall wish I had been further.

135 CAESAR: Good friends, go in and taste some wine with me,
      And we like friends will straightway go together.

      BRUTUS: *[Aside.]* That every like is not the same, O Caesar,
      The heart of Brutus yearns to think upon!
                               [Exeunt.]

SCENE 3
A street near the Capitol.

[Enter Artemidorus, reading paper.]

ARTEMIDORUS: "Caesar, beware of Brutus; take heed of Cassius;
      come not near Casca; have an eye to Cinna; trust not
      Trebonius; mark well Metellus Cimber; Decius Brutus loves
      thee not; thou hast wronged Caius Ligarius. There is but one
5   mind in all these men, and it is bent against Caesar. If thou
      beest not immortal, look about you. Security gives way to
      conspiracy. The mighty gods defend thee!
                       Thy lover, Artemidorus."
      Here will I stand till Caesar pass along,
10   And as a suitor will I give him this.
      My heart laments that virtue cannot live
      Out of the teeth of emulation.
      If thou read this, O Caesar, thou mayest live;
      If not, the Fates with traitors do contrive.   *[Exit.]*

TREBONIUS: *Caesar, I will.* [Aside.] *And I will be so near that your best friends shall wish I had been further away.*

CAESAR: Good friends, go in and taste some wine with me. We, like friends, will straightway leave together.

BRUTUS: [Aside.] The heart of Brutus yearns to think that every "like" is not the same, Oh, Caesar. [Exit.]

SCENE 3
A street near the Capitol.

[Enter Artemidorus, reading paper.]

ARTEMIDORUS: "Caesar, beware of Brutus. Take heed of Cassius. Don't come near Casca; have an eye to Cinna. Do not trust Trebonius. Watch Metellus Cimber. Decius Brutus loves you not; you have wronged Caius Ligarius. There is only one mind in all these men, and it is bent against Caesar. If you are mortal, look about you—security gives way to conspiracy. The mighty gods defend you! Your friend, Artemidorus." Here I will stand until Caesar passes by, and like a suitor I will give him this. My heart laments that your virtue cannot outshine this jealousy. If you read this, Oh, Caesar, you may yet live; if not, the fates contrive with traitors. [Exit.]

SCENE 4
Another part of the same street, before the house of Brutus.

[Enter Portia and Lucius.]

PORTIA: I prithee, boy, run to the Senate-house;
Stay not to answer me, but get thee gone.
Why dost thou stay?

LUCIUS: To know my errand, madam.

5   PORTIA: I would have had thee there, and here again,
Ere I can tell thee what thou shouldst do there.
O constancy, be strong upon my side!
Set a huge mountain 'tween my heart and tongue!
I have a man's mind, but a woman's might.
10   How hard it is for women to keep counsel!
Art thou here yet?

LUCIUS: Madam, what should I do?
Run to the Capitol, and nothing else?
And so return to you, and nothing else?

15   PORTIA: Yes, bring me word, boy, if thy lord look well,
For he went sickly forth; and take good note
What Caesar doth, what suitors press to him.
Hark, boy, what noise is that?

LUCIUS: I hear none, madam.

20   PORTIA: Prithee, listen well.
I heard a bustling rumor like a fray,
And the wind brings it from the Capitol.

LUCIUS: Sooth, madam, I hear nothing.

[Enter the Soothsayer.]

SCENE 4
Another part of the same street,
before the house of Brutus.

[Enter Portia and Lucius.]

PORTIA: I beg you, boy, run to the Senate. Do not stay another moment to answer me but get you gone. Why do you stay?

LUCIUS: To know my errand, madam.

PORTIA: I would have had you there already and back again before I can tell you what you should do there. Constancy, be strong upon my side! Set a huge mountain between my heart and my tongue! I have a man's mind but a woman's might. How hard it is for women to keep counsel! Are you still here?

LUCIUS: Madam, what should I do? Run to the Capitol and nothing else? And so return to you and nothing else?

PORTIA: Yes, bring me word, boy, if your lord looks well; for he went away looking sickly. Take good notice of what Caesar does, which suitors press him. Hark, boy, what noise is that?

LUCIUS: I hear none, madam.

PORTIA: Pray you, listen well; I heard a bustling rumor much like a battle, and it comes from the Capitol.

LUCIUS: Really, madam, I heard nothing.

[Enter the Soothsayer.]

PORTIA: Come hither, fellow; which way hast thou been?

25 SOOTHSAYER: At mine own house, good lady.

PORTIA: What is't o'clock?

SOOTHSAYER: About the ninth hour, lady.

PORTIA: Is Caesar yet gone to the Capitol?

SOOTHSAYER: Madam, not yet. I go to take my stand
30   To see him pass on to the Capitol.

PORTIA: Thou hast some suit to Caesar, hast thou not?

SOOTHSAYER: That I have, lady. If it will please Caesar
   To be so good to Caesar as to hear me,
   I shall beseech him to befriend himself.

35 PORTIA: Why, know'st thou any harm's intended towards him?

SOOTHSAYER: None that I know will be, much that I fear may
         chance.
   Good morrow to you. Here the street is narrow,
   The throng that follows Caesar at the heels,
40   Of senators, of praetors, common suitors,
   Will crowd a feeble man almost to death.
   I'll get me to a place more void and there
   Speak to great Caesar as he comes along.   *[Exit.]*

PORTIA: I must go in. Ay me, how weak a thing
45   The heart of woman is! O Brutus,
   The heavens speed thee in thine enterprise!
   Sure, the boy heard me. Brutus hath a suit
   That Caesar will not grant. O, I grow faint.
   Run, Lucius, and commend me to my lord;
50   Say I am merry. Come to me again,
   And bring me word what he doth say to thee.
                [Exeunt severally.]

PORTIA: *Come here, fellow. Where have you been?*

SOOTHSAYER: *At my own house, good lady.*

PORTIA: *What is the time?*

SOOTHSAYER: *About nine o'clock, lady.*

PORTIA: *Has Caesar arrived at the Capitol?*

SOOTHSAYER: *Not yet, madam. I'm going now to take my stand to see him pass on to the Capitol.*

PORTIA: *Do you have some request to present to Caesar?*

SOOTHSAYER: *That I have, lady. If it pleases Caesar to be so good to Caesar as to hear me, I shall beg him to be careful.*

PORTIA: *Why, do you know of any harm that is intended towards him?*

SOOTHSAYER: *None that I know for sure, but much that I fear may happen. Good morning to you. Here the street is narrow. The throng that follows Caesar at the heels—senators, praetors, common suitors—will crowd a feeble man almost to death. I'll go to a place more vacant and there speak to great Caesar as he comes along.* [Exit.]

PORTIA: *I must go in. Ah, me, how weak a thing the heart of a woman is! Brutus, the heavens speed you in your enterprise! Surely, the boy heard me. Brutus has a suit that Caesar will not grant. Oh, I grow faint. Run, Lucius, and commend me to my lord; say that I am merry. Come again to me, and bring me word what he says to you.* [Exit severally.]

85

ACT III

SCENE 1
Rome. Before the Capitol; the Senate sitting above. A crowd of people, among them Artemidorus and the Soothsayer.

[Flourish. Enter Caesar, Brutus, Cassius, Casca, Decius, Metellus, Trebonius, Cinna, Antony, Lepidus, Popilius, Publius, and others.]

CAESAR: The ides of March are come.

SOOTHSAYER: Ay, Caesar, but not gone.

ARTEMIDORUS: Hail, Caesar! Read this schedule.

DECIUS: Trebonius doth desire you to o'er read,
5   At your best leisure, this his humble suit.

ARTEMIDORUS: O Caesar, read mine first, for mine's a suit
     That touches Caesar nearer. Read it, great Caesar.

CAESAR: What touches us ourself shall be last served.

10   ARTEMIDORUS: Delay not, Caesar; read it instantly.

CAESAR: What, is the fellow mad?

PUBLIUS: Sirrah, give place.

ACT III

SCENE 1
Rome. Before the Capitol; the Senate sitting above. A crowd of people, among them Artemidorus and the Soothsayer.

[Flourish. Enter Caesar, Brutus, Cassius, Casca, Decius, Metellus, Trebonius, Cinna, Antony, Lepidus, Popilius, Publius, and others.]

CAESAR: *The fifteenth of March has come.*

SOOTHSAYER: *Ay, Caesar, but not yet gone.*

ARTEMIDORUS: *Hail, Caesar! Read this letter.*

DECIUS: *Trebonius desires that you read this, his humble suit, at your leisure.*

ARTEMIDORUS: *Oh, Caesar, read mine first. My suit touches Caesar directly. Read it, great Caesar.*

CAESAR: *What touches us ourself shall be saved for last.*

ARTEMIDORUS: *Delay not, Caesar; read it instantly.*

CAESAR: *What, is the fellow mad?*

PUBLIUS: *Sir, give us some room here.*

CASSIUS: What, urge you your petitions in the street?
  Come to the Capitol.

[Caesar goes up to the Senate-house, the rest follow.]

15 POPILIUS: I wish your enterprise today may thrive.

CASSIUS: What enterprise, Popilius?

POPILIUS: Fare you well. [Advances to Caesar.]

BRUTUS: What said Popilius Lena?

CASSIUS: He wish'd today our enterprise might thrive.
20   I fear our purpose is discovered.

BRUTUS: Look, how he makes to Caesar. Mark him.

CASSIUS: Casca,
  Be sudden, for we fear prevention.
  Brutus, what shall be done? If this be known,
25 Cassius or Caesar never shall turn back,
  For I will slay myself.

BRUTUS: Cassius, be constant.
  Popilius Lena speaks not of our purposes;
  For, look, he smiles, and Caesar doth not change.

30 CASSIUS: Trebonius knows his time, for, look you, Brutus,
  He draws Mark Antony out of the way.
                [Exeunt Antony and Trebonius.]

DECIUS: Where is Metellus Cimber? Let him go,
  And presently prefer his suit to Caesar.

BRUTUS: He is address'd; press near and second him.

35 CINNA: Casca, you are the first that rears your hand.

CASSIUS: *What, do you pass your petitions in the street? Come to the Capitol.*

[Caesar goes up to the Senate, the rest follow.]

POPILIUS: *I wish your enterprise today may thrive.*

CASSIUS: *What enterprise, Popilius?*

POPILIUS: *Farewell.* [Advances to Caesar.]

BRUTUS: *What did Popilius Lena say?*

CASSIUS: *He wished our enterprise might thrive; I fear our purpose has been discovered.*

BRUTUS: *Look, how he moves towards Caesar. Watch him.*

CASSIUS: *Casca, be sudden. I fear we have been uncovered. Brutus, what shall be done? If this is known, Cassius or Caesar will never turn back because I will slay myself.*

BRUTUS: *Cassius, be steady. Popilius Lena does not speak of our purposes. Look, he smiles, and Caesar does not change in his appearance.*

CASSIUS: *Trebonius knows his time. Look, Brutus, he draws Mark Antony out of the way.*
                                        [Exit Antony and Trebonius.]

DECIUS: *Where is Metellus Cimber? Let him go and presently offer his suit to Caesar.*

BRUTUS: *He is addressed; press near and back him up.*

CINNA: *Casca, you are the first to raise your hand.*

CAESAR: Are we all ready? What is now amiss
　　That Caesar and his Senate must redress?

METELLUS: Most high, most mighty, and most puissant Caesar,
　　Metellus Cimber throws before thy seat
40　　An humble heart.　　　　　　　　*[Kneeling.]*

CAESAR:　　　　　I must prevent thee, Cimber.
　　These couchings and these lowly courtesies
　　Might fire the blood of ordinary men
　　And turn preordinance and first decree
45　　Into the law of children. Be not fond
　　To think that Caesar bears such rebel blood
　　That will be thaw'd from the true quality
　　With that which melteth fools, I mean sweet words,
　　Low-crooked court'sies, and base spaniel-fawning.
50　　Thy brother by decree is banished.
　　If thou dost bend and pray and fawn for him,
　　I spurn thee like a cur out of my way.
　　Know, Caesar doth not wrong, nor without cause
　　Will he be satisfied.

55　　METELLUS: Is there no voice more worthy than my own,
　　To sound more sweetly in great Caesar's ear
　　For the repealing of my banish'd brother?

BRUTUS: I kiss thy hand, but not in flattery, Caesar,
　　Desiring thee that Publius Cimber may
60　　Have an immediate freedom of repeal.

CAESAR: What, Brutus?

CASSIUS:　　　　Pardon, Caesar! Caesar, pardon!
　　As low as to thy foot doth Cassius fall
　　To beg enfranchisement for Publius Cimber.

65　　CAESAR: I could be well moved, if I were as you;
　　If I could pray to move, prayers would move me;

CAESAR: *Are we all ready? What problems now need to be addressed by Caesar and his Senate?*

METELLUS: *Most high, most mighty, and most powerful Caesar, Metellus Cimber throws before your seat a humble heart—*   [Kneels.]

CAESAR: *I must stop you, Cimber. This kneeling and these bows might fire the blood of ordinary men and turn the law of the land into the law of children. Do not think, however, that Caesar bears such blood that will be thawed from the true path by that which melts fools. I refer to these sweet words, hidden in courtesies and low fawning. Your brother by decree is banished. If you continue to bend and pray and fawn for him, I ignore you like a dog in my path. Know that Caesar does not wrong you, nor will he be moved without just cause.*

METELLUS: *Is there no voice more worthy than my own to sound more sweetly in great Caesar's ear for the repealing of my brother's banishment?*

BRUTUS: *I kiss your hand, but not in flattery, Caesar. I desire that Publius Cimber may be given his freedom from banishment.*

CAESAR: *What, Brutus?*

CASSIUS: *Pardon me, Caesar! Caesar, pardon. As low as your foot do I fall to beg freedom for Publius Cimber.*

CAESAR: *If I were as you, I might be moved. If I could pray to move, prayers would move me. But I am as steady as the Northern star, whose true-*

91

But I am constant as the northern star,
Of whose true-fix'd and resting quality
There is no fellow in the firmament.
70 The skies are painted with unnumber'd sparks;
They are all fire and every one doth shine;
But there's but one in all doth hold his place.
So in the world, 'tis furnish'd well with men,
And men are flesh and blood, and apprehensive;
75 Yet in the number I do know but one
That unassailable holds on his rank,
Unshaked of motion; and that I am he,
Let me a little show it, even in this;
That I was constant Cimber should be banish'd,
80 And constant do remain to keep him so.

CINNA: O Caesar,—

CAESAR: Hence! Wilt thou lift up Olympus?

DECIUS: Great Caesar—

CAESAR: Doth not Brutus bootless kneel?

85 CASCA: Speak, hands, for me!

[Casca first, then the other Conspirators and Marcus Brutus stab
Caesar.]

CAESAR: Et tu, Brute?— Then fall, Caesar!   [Dies.]

CINNA: Liberty! Freedom! Tyranny is dead!
    Run hence, proclaim, cry it about the streets.

CASSIUS: Some to the common pulpits and cry out
90   "Liberty, freedom, and enfranchisement!"

BRUTUS: People, and senators, be not affrighted,
    Fly not, stand still; ambition's debt is paid.

92

fixed and constant quality has no equal in the world. The skies are painted with numerous sparks; they are all fire and every one does shine. But only the Northern star always holds his place. So it is in the world. It is furnished well with men, but men are flesh and blood and endowed with intelligence. Yet, in that number I do know only one who holds onto his rank without change, unshaken by motion. That is I. Let me show a little of it even in this. I was constant that Cimber should be banished, and constant I will remain to keep him so.

CINNA: *Oh, Caesar—*

CAESAR: *Away! Will you lift up Olympus, too?*

DECIUS: *Great Caesar—*

CAESAR: *Does not Brutus kneel uselessly?*

CASCA: *Hands, speak for me!*

[Casca first, then the other conspirators and Marcus Brutus stab Caesar.]

CAESAR: [Incredulous.] *And you, Brutus?—Then fall, Caesar!* [Dies.]

CINNA: *Liberty! Freedom! Tyranny is dead! Run from here and proclaim it; cry it about the streets.*

CASSIUS: *Some go to the common pulpits and cry out, "Liberty, freedom, and enfranchisement!"*

BRUTUS: *People and senators, do not be frightened. Do not flee; stand stoutly. Ambition's debt has been paid.*

93

CASCA: Go to the pulpit, Brutus.

DECIUS: And Cassius too.

95   BRUTUS: Where's Publius?

CINNA: Here, quite confounded with this mutiny.

METELLUS: Stand fast together, lest some friend of Caesar's
    Should chance—

BRUTUS: Talk not of standing. Publius, good cheer,
100   There is no harm intended to your person,
    Nor to no Roman else. So tell them, Publius.

CASSIUS: And leave us, Publius, lest that the people
    Rushing on us should do your age some mischief.

BRUTUS: Do so, and let no man abide this deed
105   But we the doers.

[Re-enter Trebonius.]

CASSIUS: Where is Antony?

TREBONIUS: Fled to his house amazed.
    Men, wives, and children stare, cry out, and run
    As it were doomsday.

110   BRUTUS: Fates, we will know your pleasures.
    That we shall die, we know; 'tis but the time
    And drawing days out that men stand upon.

CASSIUS: Why, he that cuts off twenty years of life
    Cuts off so many years of fearing death.

115   BRUTUS: Grant that, and then is death a benefit;
    So are we Caesar's friends that have abridged

CASCA: Go to the pulpit, Brutus.

DECIUS: And Cassius, too.

BRUTUS: Where's Publius?

CINNA: Here, quite confused by this mutiny.

METELLUS: Stand fast together so that some friend of Caesar's might not chance—

BRUTUS: Talk not of standing. Publius, be of good cheer; there is no harm intended to your person, nor to any other Roman. Tell them, Publius.

CASSIUS: And leave us, Publius, before the people rushing to us should do your age some harm.

BRUTUS: Do so, and let no man suffer because of this deed other than we, the doers.

[Re-enter Trebonius.]

CASSIUS: Where is Antony?

TREBONIUS: Fled to his house in amazement. Men, wives, and children stare, cry out, and run as if it were doomsday.

BRUTUS: Fates, we will know your pleasures. That we will die, we know. It is only the time and the long days that men wait for.

CASSIUS: Why, he that cuts off twenty years of life cuts off so many years of fearing death.

BRUTUS: Grant that is true, and then death is a benefit. We are Caesar's friends who have shortened his time of fearing death. Stoop, Romans,

His time of fearing death. Stoop, Romans, stoop,
And let us bathe our hands in Caesar's blood
Up to the elbows, and besmear our swords;
120   Then walk we forth, even to the market-place,
And waving our red weapons o'er our heads,
Let's all cry, "Peace, freedom, and liberty!"

CASSIUS: Stoop then, and wash. How many ages hence
Shall this our lofty scene be acted over
In states unborn and accents yet unknown!

125   BRUTUS: How many times shall Caesar bleed in sport,
That now on Pompey's basis lies along
No worthier than the dust!

CASSIUS: So oft as that shall be,
So often shall the knot of us be call'd
130   The men that gave their country liberty.

DECIUS: What, shall we forth?

CASSIUS: Ay, every man away.
Brutus shall lead, and we will grace his heels
With the most boldest and best hearts of Rome.

[Enter a Servant.]

135   BRUTUS: Soft, who comes here? A friend of Antony's.

SERVANT: Thus, Brutus, did my master bid me kneel,
Thus did Mark Antony bid me fall down,
And, being prostrate, thus he bade me say:
Brutus is noble, wise, valiant, and honest;
140   Caesar was mighty, bold, royal, and loving.
Say I love Brutus and I honor him;
Say I fear'd Caesar, honor'd him, and loved him.
If Brutus will vouchsafe that Antony
May safely come to him and be resolved

stoop, and let us bathe our hands in Caesar's blood up to the elbows and smear our swords. Then we will walk to the marketplace and, waving our red weapons over our heads, let us all cry, "Peace, freedom, and liberty!"

CASSIUS: Stoop then, and wash. How many ages in the future will reenact our high-minded scene in states unborn and accents yet unknown!

BRUTUS: How many times will Caesar bleed in reenactment; he who now on Pompey's pedestal lies alone, no worthier than the dust!

CASSIUS: As often as that happens, so too will the group of us be called the men who gave their country liberty.

DECIUS: Well, shall we go out?

CASSIUS: Yes, every man away. Brutus will lead, and we will follow him with the boldest and best hearts of Rome.

[Enter a Servant.]

BRUTUS: Easy! Who comes here? A friend of Antony's.

SERVANT: Thus, Brutus, my master asked me to kneel; thus did Mark Antony ask me to fall down. Being prone, thus he asked me to say that Brutus is noble, wise, valiant, and honest; Caesar was mighty, bold, royal, and loving. Say that I love Brutus and I honor him; say I feared Caesar, honored him, and loved him, too. If Brutus will promise that Antony might safely come to him and learn how Caesar has deserved to lie in death, then Mark Antony will not love Caesar dead as well as he loves Brutus alive. He would follow the fortunes and affairs of noble Brutus through the hazards of this newly formed state with all true faith. So says my master, Antony.

145   How Caesar hath deserved to lie in death,
Mark Antony shall not love Caesar dead
So well as Brutus living, but will follow
The fortunes and affairs of noble Brutus
Thorough the hazards of this untrod state
150   With all true faith. So says my master Antony.

BRUTUS: Thy master is a wise and valiant Roman;
I never thought him worse.
Tell him, so please him come unto this place,
He shall be satisfied and, by my honor,
155   Depart untouch'd.

SERVANT: I'll fetch him presently.   *[Exit.]*

BRUTUS: I know that we shall have him well to friend.

CASSIUS: I wish we may, but yet have I a mind
That fears him much, and my misgiving still
160   Falls shrewdly to the purpose.

[Re-enter Antony.]

BRUTUS: But here comes Antony. Welcome, Mark Antony.

ANTONY: O mighty Caesar! Dost thou lie so low?
Are all thy conquests, glories, triumphs, spoils,
Shrunk to this little measure? Fare thee well.
165   I know not, gentlemen, what you intend,
Who else must be let blood, who else is rank.
If I myself, there is no hour so fit
As Caesar's death's hour, nor no instrument
Of half that worth as those your swords, made rich
175   With the most noble blood of all this world.
I do beseech ye, if you bear me hard,
Now, whilst your purpled hands do reek and smoke,
Fulfill your pleasure. Live a thousand years,
I shall not find myself so apt to die;

BRUTUS: *Your master is a wise and valiant Roman; I never thought of him as other. Tell him to please come to this place. He will be satisfied and, by my honor, depart untouched.*

SERVANT: *I'll fetch him at once.*   [Exit.]

BRUTUS: *I know that we will have him as our good friend.*

CASSIUS: *I wish we may, but I fear him much. My misgiving is strong to that purpose.*

[Re-enter Antony.]

BRUTUS: *But here comes Antony. Welcome, Mark Antony.*

ANTONY: *Oh, mighty Caesar! Do you lie so low? Are all your conquests, glories, triumphs, and spoils shrunk to this small measure? Fare you well. I know not, gentlemen, what you intend, who else must give their blood, who else is to be killed. If I myself am one, there is no better hour than that of Caesar's death, nor any instrument half so worthy as your swords made rich with the most noble blood of all this world. I do beg you, if you want me dead, finish your task now while your stained hands reek and smoke. If I live a thousand years, I will not find myself so ready to die. No place would please me more, no means of death, as here by Caesar, and by you stabbed—you the choicest, best men of this time.*

180   No place will please me so, no mean of death,
       As here by Caesar, and by you cut off,
       The choice and master spirits of this age.

       BRUTUS: O Antony, beg not your death of us!
       Though now we must appear bloody and cruel,
185   As, by our hands and this our present act,
       You see we do, yet see you but our hands
       And this the bleeding business they have done.
       Our hearts you see not; they are pitiful;
       And pity to the general wrong of Rome—
190   As fire drives out fire, so pity pity—
       Hath done this deed on Caesar. For your part,
       To you our swords have leaden points, Mark Antony;
       Our arms in strength of malice, and our hearts
       Of brothers' temper, do receive you in
195   With all kind love, good thoughts, and reverence.

       CASSIUS: Your voice shall be as strong as any man's
       In the disposing of new dignities.

       BRUTUS: Only be patient till we have appeased
       The multitude, beside themselves with fear,
200   And then we will deliver you the cause
       Why I, that did love Caesar when I struck him,
       Have thus proceeded.

       ANTONY: I doubt not of your wisdom.
       Let each man render me his bloody hand.
205   First, Marcus Brutus, will I shake with you;
       Next, Caius Cassius, do I take your hand;
       Now, Decius Brutus, yours; now yours, Metellus;
       Yours, Cinna; and, my valiant Casca, yours;
       Though last, not least in love, yours, good Trebonius.
210   Gentlemen all,—alas, what shall I say?
       My credit now stands on such slippery ground,
       That one of two bad ways you must conceit me,
       Either a coward or a flatterer.

BRUTUS: Though we must now appear bloody and cruel, please do not beg us for your death, Antony. You see only our hands and our act of assassination. You do not see our hearts, which have taken this action to right the wrongs of Rome. We are the ones to be pitied here. We are not going to harm you, Mark Antony. You are one whom we receive in brotherhood, love, and respect.

CASSIUS: Your voice shall be as powerful as any man's in the disposing of any new honors.

BRUTUS: You must be patient until we have appeased the mob, which is beside itself with fear. Then we will deliver you the reason why I, who loved Caesar when I struck him, have proceeded in this matter.

ANTONY: I do not doubt your wisdom. Let each man give me his bloody hand. First, Marcus Brutus, will I shake with you; next, Caius Cassius, do I take your hand. Now, Decius Brutus, yours; now yours, Metellus. Yours, Cinna; and my valiant Casca, yours. Though last, not the least, yours, good Trebonius. You are all gentlemen—alas, what will I say? My good name now stands on such slippery ground that you must view me as either a coward or a flatterer. I did love you, Caesar, it is true! If your spirit can look upon us now, will it not grieve for more than just your death if it sees your Antony making his peace with your noble foes and shaking their bloody hands. And in the presence of your corpse, too? Had I as many eyes as you have wounds, weeping as fast as they stream forth

That I did love thee, Caesar, O, 'tis true!
215   If then thy spirit look upon us now,
Shall it not grieve thee dearer than thy death
To see thy Antony making his peace,
Shaking the bloody fingers of thy foes,
Most noble! In the presence of thy corse?
220   Had I as many eyes as thou hast wounds,
Weeping as fast as they stream forth thy blood,
It would become me better than to close
In terms of friendship with thine enemies.
Pardon me, Julius! Here wast thou bay'd, brave hart,
225   Here didst thou fall, and here thy hunters stand,
Sign'd in thy spoil, and crimson'd in thy lethe.
O world, thou wast the forest to this hart,
And this, indeed, O world, the heart of thee.
How like a deer strucken by many princes
230   Dost thou here lie!

CASSIUS: Mark Antony,—

ANTONY: Pardon me, Caius Cassius.
The enemies of Caesar shall say this:
Then, in a friend, it is cold modesty.

235 CASSIUS: I blame you not for praising Caesar so;
But what compact mean you to have with us?
Will you be prick'd in number of our friends,
Or shall we on, and not depend on you?

ANTONY: Therefore I took your hands, but was indeed
240   Sway'd from the point by looking down on Caesar.
Friends am I with you all and love you all,
Upon this hope that you shall give me reasons
Why and wherein Caesar was dangerous.

BRUTUS: Or else were this a savage spectacle.
245   Our reasons are so full of good regard
That were you, Antony, the son of Caesar,
You should be satisfied.

ACT III SCENE 1

your blood, it would become me better than to join in friendship with your enemies. Pardon me, Julius! Here was the spot where you were cornered, brave deer. Here you fell and here your hunters stand covered with your life's blood. World, you were the forest to this deer. Indeed, this is truly how your life was ended. How like a deer struck by many princes do you lie here!

CASSIUS: *Mark Antony —*

ANTONY: *Pardon me, Caius Cassius. The enemies of Caesar will say this. For a friend to say this is not excessive.*

CASSIUS: *I do not blame you for praising Caesar highly; but what agreement do you mean to have with us? Will you be placed in the number of our friends, or we move on and not depend on you?*

ANTONY: *I took your hands but was indeed moved from that point by looking down on Caesar's body. I am your friend and love you all if you can give me reasons why and how Caesar was dangerous.*

BRUTUS: *This would be savage spectacle otherwise. Our reasons are so full of thoughtfulness that were you, Antony, the son of Caesar, you would be satisfied.*

103

ANTONY: That's all I seek;
    And am moreover suitor that I may
250   Produce his body to the marketplace,
    And in the pulpit, as becomes a friend,
    Speak in the order of his funeral.

BRUTUS: You shall, Mark Antony.

CASSIUS: Brutus, a word with you.
255   *[Aside to Brutus.]* You know not what you do. Do not consent
    That Antony speak in his funeral.
    Know you how much the people may be moved
    By that which he will utter?

BRUTUS: By your pardon,
260   I will myself into the pulpit first,
    And show the reason of our Caesar's death.
    What Antony shall speak, I will protest
    He speaks by leave and by permission,
    And that we are contented Caesar shall
265   Have all true rites and lawful ceremonies.
    It shall advantage more than do us wrong.

CASSIUS: I know not what may fall; I like it not.

BRUTUS: Mark Antony, here, take you Caesar's body.
    You shall not in your funeral speech blame us,
270   But speak all good you can devise of Caesar,
    And say you do't by our permission,
    Else shall you not have any hand at all
    About his funeral. And you shall speak
    In the same pulpit whereto I am going,
275   After my speech is ended.

ANTONY: Be it so,
    I do desire no more.

ANTONY: *That is all I seek; and if I may, I ask that you allow me to carry Caesar's body to the market and address the assembled crowd from the pulpit.*

BRUTUS: *You may, Mark Antony.*

CASSIUS: *Brutus, a word with you.* [Aside to Brutus.]
You don't know what you are doing. Do not consent to Antony speaking at Caesar's funeral. Do you not know how much the people may be moved by what he will say?

BRUTUS: *Excuse me, but I will myself go to the pulpit first and show the reason why we killed Caesar. Before Antony speaks, I will announce that he speaks by our leave and by our permission and that we are agreed that Caesar will have all true rites and lawful ceremonies. It will be to our advantage rather than to do us wrong.*

CASSIUS: *I do not know what will happen, but I don't like it.*

BRUTUS: *Mark Antony, here, take Caesar's body. You shall not blame us in your funeral speech. Rather, speak all good that you can devise of Caesar; and say you do it by our permission. Otherwise, you will not have any hand at all in his funeral. You shall speak in the same pulpit where I am going, but only after my speech has ended.*

ANTONY: *Be it so. I desire no more.*

BRUTUS: Prepare the body then, and follow us.

[Exeunt all but Antony.]

ANTONY: O, pardon me, thou bleeding piece of earth,
280   That I am meek and gentle with these butchers!
    Thou art the ruins of the noblest man
    That ever lived in the tide of times.
    Woe to the hand that shed this costly blood!
    Over thy wounds now do I prophesy
285   Which like dumb mouths do ope their ruby lips
    To beg the voice and utterance of my tongue,
    A curse shall light upon the limbs of men;
    Domestic fury and fierce civil strife
    Shall cumber all the parts of Italy;
290   Blood and destruction shall be so in use,
    And dreadful objects so familiar,
    That mothers shall but smile when they behold
    Their infants quarter'd with the hands of war;
    All pity choked with custom of fell deeds,
295   And Caesar's spirit ranging for revenge,
    With Ate by his side come hot from hell,
    Shall in these confines with a monarch's voice
    Cry "Havoc!" and let slip the dogs of war,
    That this foul deed shall smell above the earth
300   With carrion men, groaning for burial.

[Enter a Servant.]
    You serve Octavius Caesar, do you not?

SERVANT: I do, Mark Antony.

ANTONY: Caesar did write for him to come to Rome.

SERVANT: He did receive his letters, and is coming,
305   And bid me say to you by word of mouth—
    O Caesar!   *[Sees the body.]*

BRUTUS: *Prepare the body then, and follow us.*
        [Exit all but Antony, who stands by Caesar's body.]

ANTONY: *Oh, pardon me, you bleeding piece of earth, that I am meek and gentle with these butchers! You are the ruins of the noblest man that ever lived in the history of the world. Woe to the hand that shed this costly blood! Over thy wounds now do I promise—which like mute mouths do open their ruby lips to beg the voice and utterance of my tongue—a curse shall fall upon the limbs of men. Domestic fury and fierce civil war shall entangle all parts of Italy. Blood and destruction shall be so common and dreadful objects so familiar that mothers will only smile when they behold their infants killed by the hands of war. All pity will be smothered with the doing of foul deeds. Caesar's spirit, ranging for revenge with Ate by his side hot from hell, will in these confines with a monarch's voice cry, "Havoc!" and let loose the dogs of war. This foul deed shall cause the earth to swell with dying men, groaning for burial.*

[Enter a Servant.]
    You serve Octavius Caesar, do you not?

SERVANT: *I do, Mark Antony.*

ANTONY: *Caesar wrote for him to come to Rome.*

SERVANT: *He received his letters and is coming; he bid me say to you by word of mouth—Oh, Caesar!*   [Sees the body.]

ANTONY: Thy heart is big; get thee apart and weep.
Passion, I see, is catching, for mine eyes,
Seeing those beads of sorrow stand in thine,
310   Began to water. Is thy master coming?

SERVANT: He lies tonight within seven leagues of Rome.

ANTONY: Post back with speed and tell him what hath chanced.
Here is a mourning Rome, a dangerous Rome,
No Rome of safety for Octavius yet;
315   Hie hence, and tell him so. Yet stay awhile,
Thou shalt not back till I have borne this corse
Into the market-place. There shall I try,
In my oration, how the people take
The cruel issue of these bloody men,
320   According to the which thou shalt discourse
To young Octavius of the state of things.
Lend me your hand.   *[Exeunt with Caesar's body.]*

SCENE 2
The Forum.

[Enter Brutus and Cassius, and a throng of Citizens.]

CITIZENS: We will be satisfied! Let us be satisfied!

BRUTUS: Then follow me and give me audience, friends.
Cassius, go you into the other street
And part the numbers.
5   Those that will hear me speak, let 'em stay here;
Those that will follow Cassius, go with him;
And public reasons shall be rendered
Of Caesar's death.

FIRST CITIZEN: I will hear Brutus speak.

ANTONY: *Your heart is big; get alone and weep. Passion, I see, is catching; for my eyes, seeing those beads of sorrow stand in yours, began to water. Is your master coming?*

SERVANT: *He lies tonight within twenty miles of Rome.*

ANTONY: *Go back with speed and tell him what has happened. Here is a mourning Rome, a dangerous Rome—no Rome of safety for Octavius yet. Go there, and tell him so. Yet stay awhile. You will not go back until I have carried this corpse into the marketplace. There I will give my oration. Let Octavius know how the crowd receives and responds to my speech about the murder of Caesar. Give me your hand.*

[Exit with Caesar's body.]

SCENE 2
The Forum.

[Enter Brutus and Cassius, and a throng of Citizens.]

CITIZENS: *We will be satisfied! Let us be satisfied!*

BRUTUS: *Then follow me and give me time to speak, friends. Cassius, go into the other street and divide the people there. Those who will hear me speak, let them stay here; those who will follow Cassius, go with him. Public reasons will be given as to the cause of Caesar's death.*

FIRST CITIZEN: *I will hear Brutus speak.*

10   SECOND CITIZEN: I will hear Cassius and compare their reasons,
        When severally we hear them rendered.
                *[Exit Cassius, with some of the Citizens. Brutus goes into
                the pulpit.]*

     THIRD CITIZEN: The noble Brutus is ascended. Silence!

     BRUTUS: Be patient till the last.
        Romans, countrymen, and lovers! Hear me for my cause, and
15   be silent, that you may hear. Believe me for mine honor, and
        have respect to mine honor, that you may believe. Censure me
        in your wisdom, and awake your senses, that you may the
        better judge. If there be any in this assembly, any dear friend
        of Caesar's, to him I say that Brutus' love to Caesar was no
20   less than his. If then that friend demand why Brutus rose
        against Caesar, this is my answer: Not that I loved Caesar less,
        but that I loved Rome more. Had you rather Caesar were
        living and die all slaves, than that Caesar were dead to live all
        freemen? As Caesar loved me, I weep for him; as he was for-
25   tunate, I rejoice at it; as he was valiant, I honor him; but as he
        was ambitious, I slew him. There is tears for his love, joy for
        his fortune, honor for his valor, and death for his ambition.
        Who is here so base that would be a bondman? If any, speak,
        for him have I offended. Who is here so rude that would not
30   be a Roman? If any, speak, for him have I offended. Who is
        here so vile that will not love his country? If any, speak, for
        him have I offended. I pause for a reply.

     ALL: None, Brutus, none.

     BRUTUS: Then none have I offended. I have done no more to
35   Caesar than you shall do to Brutus. The question of his death
        is enrolled in the Capitol, his glory not extenuated, wherein
        he was worthy, nor his offenses enforced, for which he suf-
        fered death.

     [Enter Antony and others, with Caesar's body.]
        Here comes his body, mourned by Mark Antony, who, though

110

SECOND CITIZEN: *I will hear Cassius, and we may compare their reasons once all the reasons are put forth.*

[Exit Cassius, with some Citizens. Brutus goes into the pulpit.]

THIRD CITIZEN: *The noble Brutus has climbed the stairs. Silence!*

BRUTUS: *Be patient until the end. Romans, countrymen, and friends! Hear me for my cause. Be quiet, that you may hear me. Believe me because of my honor, and have respect for my honor to listen to what I have to say. Judge me in your wisdom, and awake your senses so that you may judge me the better. If there is any one in this assembly, any dear friend of Caesar's, to him I say that Brutus' love for Caesar was no less than yours. If that friend then demands why Brutus rose against Caesar, this is my answer—not that I loved Caesar less but that I loved Rome more. Would you rather that Caesar were living and all of us die slaves; rather than that Caesar were dead, and all of us live as free men? As Caesar loved me, I weep for him; as he was fortunate, I rejoice; as he was valiant, I honor him. But as he was ambitious, I slew him. There are tears for his love, joy for his fortune, honor for his valor, and death for his ambition. Who is here so low that he would be a slave? If there is any, speak now; for I have offended him. Who is here so unsophisticated that he would not be a Roman? If there is any, speak now; for I have offended him. Who is here so wicked that he would not love his country? If there is any, speak now; for I have offended him. I pause for a reply.*

ALL: *None, Brutus. None.*

BRUTUS: *Then I have offended none. I have done no more to Caesar than you shall do to Brutus. The reasons for his death are recorded in the Capitol. His achievements have not been slighted, nor the crimes for which he was killed exaggerated.*

[Enter Antony and others, with Caesar's body.]
Here comes his body, mourned by Mark Antony who, though he had no

111

40   he had no hand in his death, shall receive the benefit of his
      dying, a place in the commonwealth, as which of you shall
      not? With this I depart—that, as I slew my best lover for the
      good of Rome, I have the same dagger for myself, when it
      shall please my country to need my death.

45   ALL : Live, Brutus, live, live!

      FIRST CITIZEN: Bring him with triumph home unto his house.

      SECOND CITIZEN: Give him a statue with his ancestors.

      THIRD CITIZEN: Let him be Caesar.

      FOURTH CITIZEN: Caesar's better parts
50   Shall be crown'd in Brutus.

      FIRST CITIZEN: We'll bring him to his house with shouts and
         clamors.

      BRUTUS: My countrymen—

      SECOND CITIZEN: Peace! Silence! Brutus speaks.

55   FIRST CITIZEN: Peace, ho!

      BRUTUS: Good countrymen, let me depart alone,
         And, for my sake, stay here with Antony.
         Do grace to Caesar's corse, and grace his speech
         Tending to Caesar's glories, which Mark Antony,
60   By our permission, is allow'd to make.
         I do entreat you, not a man depart,
         Save I alone, till Antony have spoke.   [Exit.]

      FIRST CITIZEN: Stay, ho, and let us hear Mark Antony.

      THIRD CITIZEN: Let him go up into the public chair;
65   We'll hear him. Noble Antony, go up.

112

hand in his death, shall receive the benefit of Caesar's death— a place in the commonwealth as all of you shall receive. With this I depart. As I slew the most noble Caesar for the good of Rome, I have the same dagger for myself when it pleases my country to need my death.

ALL: Live, Brutus! Live, live!

FIRST CITIZEN: Bring him home with triumph to his house.

SECOND CITIZEN: Give him a statue with his ancestors.

THIRD CITIZEN: Let him be Caesar.

FOURTH CITIZEN: Caesar's better parts shall be crowned in Brutus.

FIRST CITIZEN: We'll bring him to his house with shouts and clamors.

BRUTUS: My countrymen—

SECOND CITIZEN: Peace, silence! Brutus speaks.

FIRST CITIZEN: Peace, ho!

BRUTUS: Good countrymen, let me depart alone. For my sake, stay here with Antony. Honor Caesar's corpse and honor Antony's speech, which lists Caesar's glories. Mark Antony is allowed to make it with our permission. I ask that not a man depart except me alone until Antony has spoken.   [Exit.]

FIRST CITIZEN: Stay, now! Let us hear Mark Antony.

THIRD CITIZEN: Let him go up into the public chair; we'll hear him. Noble Antony, go up.

ANTONY: For Brutus' sake, I am beholding to you.

[Goes into the pulpit.]

FOURTH CITIZEN: What does he say of Brutus?

THIRD CITIZEN:　　　　He says, for Brutus' sake,
　He finds himself beholding to us all.

70　FOURTH CITIZEN: 'Twere best he speak no harm of Brutus here.

FIRST CITIZEN: This Caesar was a tyrant.

THIRD CITIZEN:　　　　　　Nay, that's certain.
　We are blest that Rome is rid of him.

SECOND CITIZEN: Peace! Let us hear what Antony can say.

75　ANTONY: You gentle Romans—

ALL:　　　　　Peace, ho! Let us hear him.

ANTONY: Friends, Romans, countrymen, lend me your ears!
　I come to bury Caesar, not to praise him.
　The evil that men do lives after them,
80　The good is oft interred with their bones;
　So let it be with Caesar. The noble Brutus
　Hath told you Caesar was ambitious;
　If it were so, it was a grievous fault,
　And grievously hath Caesar answer'd it.
85　Here, under leave of Brutus and the rest—
　For Brutus is an honorable man;
　So are they all, all honorable men—
　Come I to speak in Caesar's funeral.
　He was my friend, faithful and just to me;
90　But Brutus says he was ambitious,
　And Brutus is an honorable man.
　He hath brought many captives home to Rome,
　Whose ransoms did the general coffers fill.

ANTONY: *For Brutus' sake, I give you thanks.*

[Goes into the pulpit.]

FOURTH CITIZEN: *What does he say of Brutus?*

THIRD CITIZEN: *He says, for Brutus' sake, he finds himself beholding to us all.*

FOURTH CITIZEN: *It were best that he speaks no evil of Brutus here.*

FIRST CITIZEN: *This Caesar was a tyrant.*

THIRD CITIZEN: *Yes, that's certain. We are blessed that Rome is rid of him.*

SECOND CITIZEN: *Quiet! Let us hear what Antony says.*

ANTONY: *You gentle Romans—*

ALL: *Quiet, now! Let us hear him.*

ANTONY: *Friends, Romans, countrymen, lend me your ears; I come to bury Caesar, not to praise him. Remember that the evil that men do lives after them but the good is often buried with their bones. So let this be done with Caesar. The noble Brutus has told you Caesar was ambitious. If it were so, it was a serious fault; and seriously has Caesar answered for it. Here, with the permission of Brutus and the rest—for Brutus is an honorable man; so are they all, all honorable men—I come to speak at Caesar's funeral. He was my friend, faithful and just to me. But Brutus says he was ambitious; and Brutus is an honorable man. Caesar brought many captives home to Rome whose ransoms filled the general coffers. Did this seem ambitious in Caesar? When the poor have cried, Caesar has wept—ambition should be made of tougher stuff. Yet Brutus says he was ambitious, and Brutus is an honorable man. You all did see that on the Lupercal three times I presented him a kingly crown, which he did three times refuse. Was this ambition? Yet Brutus says he was ambitious, and surely he is an honorable man. I speak not to disprove what Brutus spoke here, but I am here to speak what I do know. You all did love*

115

Did this in Caesar seem ambitious?
95   When that the poor have cried, Caesar hath wept;
Ambition should be made of sterner stuff:
Yet Brutus says he was ambitious,
And Brutus is an honorable man.
You all did see that on the Lupercal
100   I thrice presented him a kingly crown,
Which he did thrice refuse. Was this ambition?
Yet Brutus says he was ambitious,
And sure he is an honorable man.
I speak not to disprove what Brutus spoke,
105   But here I am to speak what I do know.
You all did love him once, not without cause;
What cause withholds you then to mourn for him?
O judgement, thou art fled to brutish beasts,
And men have lost their reason. Bear with me;
110   My heart is in the coffin there with Caesar,
And I must pause till it come back to me.

FIRST CITIZEN: Methinks there is much reason in his sayings.

SECOND CITIZEN: If thou consider rightly of the matter,
Caesar has had great wrong.

115   THIRD CITIZEN: Has he, masters?
I fear there will a worse come in his place.

FOURTH CITIZEN: Mark'd ye his words? He would not take the
                crown;
Therefore 'tis certain he was not ambitious.

120   FIRST CITIZEN: If it be found so, some will dear abide it.

SECOND CITIZEN: Poor soul, his eyes are red as fire with weeping.

THIRD CITIZEN: There's not a nobler man in Rome than Antony.

FOURTH CITIZEN: Now mark him, he begins again to speak.

Caesar once and certainly not without reason. What stops you then from mourning him? Oh, judgment! You no longer hold power over men's reason. Bear with me; my heart lies in the coffin there with Caesar, and I must pause until it comes back to me.

FIRST CITIZEN: *I think there is much reason in his thoughts.*

SECOND CITIZEN: *If you consider intelligently of this matter, Caesar has had a great wrong done to him.*

THIRD CITIZEN: *Has he, masters? I fear there will be someone worse to take his place.*

FOURTH CITIZEN: *Did you listen carefully? He would not take the crown; therefore, it is certain that he was not ambitious.*

FIRST CITIZEN: *If it is found to be so, some will pay dearly for it.*

SECOND CITIZEN: *Poor soul! His eyes are red as fire with weeping.*

THIRD CITIZEN: *There's not a nobler man in Rome than Antony.*

FOURTH CITIZEN: *Pay attention; he begins to speak again.*

ANTONY: But yesterday the word of Caesar might
125   Have stood against the world. Now lies he there,
And none so poor to do him reverence.
O masters! If I were disposed to stir
Your hearts and minds to mutiny and rage,
I should do Brutus wrong and Cassius wrong,
130   Who, you all know, are honorable men.
I will not do them wrong; I rather choose
To wrong the dead, to wrong myself and you,
Than I will wrong such honorable men.
But here's a parchment with the seal of Caesar;
135   I found it in his closet, 'tis his will.
Let but the commons hear this testament—
Which, pardon me, I do not mean to read—
And they would go and kiss dead Caesar's wounds
And dip their napkins in his sacred blood,
140   Yea, beg a hair of him for memory,
And, dying, mention it within their wills,
Bequeathing it as a rich legacy
Unto their issue.

FOURTH CITIZEN: We'll hear the will. Read it, Mark Antony.

145 ALL: The will, the will! We will hear Caesar's will.

ANTONY: Have patience, gentle friends, I must not read it;
It is not meet you know how Caesar loved you.
You are not wood, you are not stones, but men;
And, being men, hearing the will of Caesar,
150   It will inflame you, it will make you mad.
'Tis good you know not that you are his heirs,
For if you should, O, what would come of it!

FOURTH CITIZEN: Read the will; we'll hear it, Antony.
You shall read us the will, Caesar's will.

155 ANTONY: Will you be patient? Will you stay a while?
I have o'ershot myself to tell you of it.

ANTONY: *Only yesterday the word of Caesar might have stood against the world; now he lies there with no one to do him reverence. Masters, if I were trying to stir your hearts and minds to mutiny and rage, I should do Brutus wrong and Cassius wrong, who—as you all know—are honorable men. I will not do them wrong. I would rather choose to wrong the dead, to wrong myself and you, rather than wrong such honorable men. But, here's a parchment with the seal of Caesar. I found it in his closet; it is his will. Let the commoners but hear this testament—which, pardon me, I do not mean to read—and they would go and kiss dead Caesar's wounds and dip their handkerchiefs into his sacred blood. Yes, they would beg for a hair of him for a remembrance which they would leave in their own wills as prized possessions for their children.*

FOURTH CITIZEN: *We'll hear the will. Read it, Mark Antony.*

ALL: *The will, the will! We will hear Caesar's will.*

ANTONY: *Have patience, good friends, I must not read it. It is not well for you to know how much Caesar loved you. You are not wood, you are not stones, but men; and, being men, hearing the will of Caesar will inflame you and make you mad. It is good that you do not know that you are his heirs. For if you should, what would come of it!*

FOURTH CITIZEN: *Read the will. We'll hear it, Antony. You must read us the will—Caesar's will.*

ANTONY: *Will you be patient? Will you stay awhile? I have overstepped my office by telling you of it. I fear that I wrong the honorable men whose daggers have stabbed Caesar. I do fear it.*

I fear I wrong the honorable men
Whose daggers have stabb'd Caesar; I do fear it.

FOURTH CITIZEN: They were traitors. "Honorable men!"

160   ALL: The will! The testament!

SECOND CITIZEN: They were villains, murderers. The will!
Read the will!

ANTONY: You will compel me then to read the will?
Then make a ring about the corse of Caesar,
165   And let me show you him that made the will.
Shall I descend? And will you give me leave?

ALL: Come down.

SECOND CITIZEN: Descend.
                        [He comes down from the pulpit.]

THIRD CITIZEN: You shall have leave.

175   FOURTH CITIZEN: A ring, stand round.

FIRST CITIZEN: Stand from the hearse, stand from the body.

SECOND CITIZEN: Room for Antony, most noble Antony.

ANTONY: Nay, press not so upon me, stand far off.

ALL: Stand back; room, bear back!

180   ANTONY: If you have tears, prepare to shed them now.
You all do know this mantle. I remember
The first time ever Caesar put it on;
'Twas on a summer's evening, in his tent,
185   That day he overcame the Nervii.
Look, in this place ran Cassius' dagger through;

FOURTH CITIZEN: *They were traitors—not honorable men!*

ALL: *The will! The testament!*

SECOND CITIZEN: *They were villains and murderers. The will! Read the will!*

ANTONY: *You will force me to read the will? Then make a ring about the corpse of Caesar, and let me show you he who made that will. Am I to descend? Will you allow me to?*

ALL: *Come down.*

SECOND CITIZEN: *Descend.*
[He comes down from the pulpit.]

THIRD CITIZEN: *You have our permission.*

FOURTH CITIZEN: *A ring, stand around in a ring.*

FIRST CITIZEN: *Stand away from the hearse; stand back from the body.*

SECOND CITIZEN: *Make room for Antony—most noble Antony.*

ANTONY: *Stop. Don't press so on me; stand far off.*

ALL: *Stand back; make room; move back!*

ANTONY: *If you have any tears, prepare to shed them now. You all do know this cloak. I remember the first time that Caesar ever put it on. It was on a summer's evening in his tent, on the day he overcame the Nervii. Look, through this place ran Cassius' dagger. See what a tear the envious Casca made. Through this cut the well-beloved Brutus stabbed. And as he moved his cursed steel away, see how the blood of Caesar followed*

See what a rent the envious Casca made;
Through this the well-beloved Brutus stabb'd;
And as he pluck'd his cursed steel away,
190 Mark how the blood of Caesar follow'd it,
As rushing out of doors, to be resolved
If Brutus so unkindly knock'd, or no;
For Brutus, as you know, was Caesar's angel.
Judge, O you gods, how dearly Caesar loved him!
195 This was the most unkindest cut of all;
For when the noble Caesar saw him stab,
Ingratitude, more strong than traitors' arms,
Quite vanquish'd him. Then burst his mighty heart,
And, in his mantle muffling up his face,
200 Even at the base of Pompey's statue,
Which all the while ran blood, great Caesar fell.
O, what a fall was there, my countrymen!
Then I, and you, and all of us fell down,
Whilst bloody treason flourish'd over us.
205 O, now you weep, and I perceive you feel
The dint of pity. These are gracious drops.
Kind souls, what weep you when you but behold
Our Caesar's vesture wounded? Look you here,
Here is himself, marr'd, as you see, with traitors.

210 FIRST CITIZEN: O piteous spectacle!

SECOND CITIZEN: O noble Caesar!

THIRD CITIZEN: O woeful day!

FOURTH CITIZEN: O traitors, villains!

FIRST CITIZEN: O most bloody sight!

215 SECOND CITIZEN: We will be revenged.

ALL: Revenge! About! Seek! Burn! Fire! Kill!
Slay! Let not a traitor live!

it as if it were rushing out to see if it really was Brutus who had cut Caesar. No, it can't be Brutus; for as you know, he was Caesar's angel. Judge, you gods, how enormously Caesar loved him! This was the unkindest cut of all. When the noble Caesar saw him stab, the ingratitude, much stronger than traitors' arms, quite came over him. Then his mighty heart burst. With his mantle muffling up to his face and with blood flowing freely, he fell at the base of Pompey's statue. What a fall that was, my countrymen! Then I and you and all of us fell down also, while bloody treason flourished over us. Now you weep, and I perceive you feel the hint of pity. Are these gracious drops indeed kind souls which you weep when you behold our Caesar's body so wounded? Look you here—here is Caesar, destroyed, as you see, by traitors.

FIRST CITIZEN: Oh, piteous spectacle!

SECOND CITIZEN: Oh, noble Caesar!

THIRD CITIZEN: Oh, woeful is the day!

FOURTH CITIZEN: Oh, traitors, villains!

FIRST CITIZEN: Oh, most bloody sight!

SECOND CITIZEN: We will be revenged.

ALL: Revenge! Move! Seek! Burn! Fire! Kill! Destroy! Let not a traitor live!

ANTONY: Stay, countrymen.

FIRST CITIZEN: Peace there! Hear the noble Antony.

220 SECOND CITIZEN: We'll hear him, we'll follow him, we'll die with
him.

ANTONY: Good friends, sweet friends, let me not stir you up
To such a sudden flood of mutiny.
They that have done this deed are honorable.
225 What private griefs they have, alas, I know not,
That made them do it. They are wise and honorable,
And will, no doubt, with reasons answer you.
I come not, friends, to steal away your hearts.
I am no orator, as Brutus is;
230 But, as you know me all, a plain blunt man,
That love my friend, and that they know full well
That gave me public leave to speak of him.
For I have neither wit, nor words, nor worth,
Action, nor utterance, nor the power of speech,
235 To stir men's blood. I only speak right on;
I tell you that which you yourselves do know;
Show you sweet Caesar's wounds, poor poor dumb mouths,
And bid them speak for me. But were I Brutus,
And Brutus Antony, there were an Antony
240 Would ruffle up your spirits and put a tongue
In every wound of Caesar that should move
The stones of Rome to rise and mutiny.

ALL: We'll mutiny.

FIRST CITIZEN: We'll burn the house of Brutus.

245 THIRD CITIZEN: Away, then! Come, seek the conspirators.

ANTONY: Yet hear me, countrymen; yet hear me speak.

ALL: Peace, ho! Hear Antony, most noble Antony!

124

ANTONY: *Wait, countrymen.*

FIRST CITIZEN: *Peace there! Hear the noble Antony.*

SECOND CITIZEN: *We'll hear him; we'll follow him; we'll die with him.*

ANTONY: *Good friends, sweet friends, let me not stir you up to such a sudden flurry of mutiny. They that have done this deed are honorable. What private matters they have unresolved, alas, which made them do it, I do not know. They are wise and honorable and will, no doubt, answer you with reasonable arguments. I come not, friends, to steal away your hearts. I am not an orator as Brutus is. But, as you all know me, I am a plain, direct man who loved his friend. Those who allowed me to speak know full well that I have neither wit, nor words, nor worth, nor action, nor utterance, nor the power of speech to stir a man's blood. I speak plainly only to the facts. I tell you that which you yourselves know already. I can show you sweet Caesar's wounds, which are like mouths which could speak for me. But if I were Brutus and Brutus were Antony, there would be an Antony who would shake your spirits and put a tongue in every wound of Caesar that would move even the stones of Rome to rise and mutiny.*

ALL: *We'll mutiny.*

FIRST CITIZEN: *We'll burn down the house of Brutus.*

THIRD CITIZEN: *Away, then! Come; find the conspirators.*

ANTONY: *Yet hear me, countrymen; yet hear me speak.*

ALL: *Quiet, now! Hear Antony, most noble Antony!*

125

ANTONY: Why, friends, you go to do you know not what.
　　Wherein hath Caesar thus deserved your loves?
250　Alas, you know not; I must tell you then.
　　You have forgot the will I told you of.

ALL : Most true, the will! Let's stay and hear the will.

ANTONY: Here is the will, and under Caesar's seal.
　　To every Roman citizen he gives,
255　To every several man, seventy-five drachmas.

SECOND CITIZEN: Most noble Caesar! We'll revenge his death.

THIRD CITIZEN: O royal Caesar!

ANTONY: Hear me with patience.

ALL : Peace, ho!

260　ANTONY: Moreover, he hath left you all his walks,
　　His private arbors, and new-planted orchards,
　　On this side Tiber; he hath left them you,
　　And to your heirs for ever; common pleasures,
　　To walk abroad and recreate yourselves.
265　Here was a Caesar! When comes such another?

FIRST CITIZEN: Never, never. Come, away, away!
　　We'll burn his body in the holy place
　　And with the brands fire the traitors' houses.
　　Take up the body.

270　SECOND CITIZEN: Go fetch fire.

THIRD CITIZEN: Pluck down benches.

FOURTH CITIZEN: Pluck down forms, windows, any thing.
　　　　　　　　　　　[Exeunt Citizens with the body.]

ANTONY: Why, friends, you don't know why you are going. Why does Caesar deserve such a love? Alas, you don't know. I must tell you then. You have forgotten Caesar's will.

ALL: Indeed, we have. The will! Let's stay a bit and hear the will.

ANTONY: Here is the will still graced by Caesar's seal. He gives to every Roman citizen, every man, seventy-five drachmas.

SECOND CITIZEN: Most noble Caesar! We'll revenge his death.

THIRD CITIZEN: Oh, royal Caesar!

ANTONY: Hear me with patience.

ALL: Quiet, now!

ANTONY: Moreover, he has also left you all of his parks, gardens, and new-planted orchards on this side of the river. He has left them to you and to your heirs forever—common pleasures to walk about in and relax in. Here was a Caesar! When will another come such as he?

FIRST CITIZEN: Never, never! Come. Away, away! We'll burn his body in the holy place, and with the kindling fire we'll burn the traitors' houses. Take up the body.

SECOND CITIZEN: Go fetch some fire.

THIRD CITIZEN: Throw down the benches.

FOURTH CITIZEN: Throw down forms, windows— anything.
                              [Exit Citizens with the body.]

ANTONY: Now let it work. Mischief, thou art afoot,
    Take thou what course thou wilt.

[Enter a Servant.]
275   How now, fellow?

SERVANT: Sir, Octavius is already come to Rome.

ANTONY: Where is he?

SERVANT: He and Lepidus are at Caesar's house.

ANTONY: And thither will I straight to visit him.
280   He comes upon a wish. Fortune is merry,
    And in this mood will give us any thing.

SERVANT: I heard him say, Brutus and Cassius
    Are rid like madmen through the gates of Rome.

ANTONY: Belike they had some notice of the people,
285   How I had moved them. Bring me to Octavius.
                                                [Exeunt.]

ANTONY: *Now let it work. Mischief, you are about; take whatever course you will.*

[Enter a Servant.]
   Well, fellow?

SERVANT: *Sir. Octavius is already in Rome.*

ANTONY: *Where is he?*

SERVANT: *He and Lepidus are at Caesar's house.*

ANTONY: *And I will straight away to visit him. He comes as an answer to my wish. Fortune is on our side and, in this mood, will give us anything.*

SERVANT: *I heard him say that Brutus and Cassius rode like madmen out of the gates of Rome.*

ANTONY: *They probably heard that I had stirred the people. Bring me to Octavius.*   [Exit.]

SCENE 3
A street.

[Enter Cinna the poet.]

CINNA: I dreamt tonight that I did feast with Caesar,
 And things unluckily charge my fantasy.
 I have no will to wander forth of doors,
 Yet something leads me forth.

[Enter Citizens.]

5   FIRST CITIZEN: What is your name?

SECOND CITIZEN: Whither are you going?

THIRD CITIZEN: Where do you dwell?

FOURTH CITIZEN: Are you a married man or a bachelor?

SECOND CITIZEN: Answer every man directly.

10   FIRST CITIZEN: Ay, and briefly.

FOURTH CITIZEN: Ay, and wisely.

THIRD CITIZEN: Ay, and truly, you were best.

CINNA: What is my name? Whither am I going? Where do I
 dwell? Am I a married man or a bachelor? Then, to answer
15   every man directly and briefly, wisely and truly: wisely I say, I
 am a bachelor.

SECOND CITIZEN: That's as much as to say, they are fools that
 marry. You'll bear me a bang for that, I fear. Proceed directly.

CINNA: Directly, I am going to Caesar's funeral.

SCENE 3
A street.

[Enter Cinna the poet.]

CINNA: I dreamed tonight that I feasted with Caesar, and unlucky things fill my imagination. I have no desire to wander out of doors, yet something leads me to do so.

[Enter Citizens.]

FIRST CITIZEN: What is your name?

SECOND CITIZEN: Where are you going?

THIRD CITIZEN: Where do you live?

FOURTH CITIZEN: Are you a married man or a bachelor?

SECOND CITIZEN: Directly answer every man.

FIRST CITIZEN: Yes, and briefly.

FOURTH CITIZEN: Yes, and wisely.

THIRD CITIZEN: Yes, and truly, if you know what is good for you.

CINNA: What is my name? Where am I going? Where do I live? Am I a married man or a bachelor? To answer every man directly and briefly, wisely and truly. Well, wisely I say, I am a bachelor.

SECOND CITIZEN: That's as much as to say that they are fools who marry. You'll be beaten for that, I think. Proceed directly.

CINNA: Directly, I am going to Caesar's funeral.

20   FIRST CITIZEN: As a friend or an enemy?

CINNA: As a friend.

SECOND CITIZEN: That matter is answered directly.

FOURTH CITIZEN: For your dwelling, briefly.

CINNA: Briefly, I dwell by the Capitol.

25   THIRD CITIZEN: Your name, sir, truly.

CINNA: Truly, my name is Cinna.

FIRST CITIZEN: Tear him to pieces, he's a conspirator.

CINNA: I am Cinna the poet, I am Cinna the poet.

FOURTH CITIZEN: Tear him for his bad verses, tear him
30   for his bad verses.

CINNA: I am not Cinna the conspirator.

FOURTH CITIZEN: It is no matter, his name's Cinna. Pluck but his
name out of his heart, and turn him going.

THIRD CITIZEN: Tear him, tear him! Come, brands, ho, firebrands.
35   To Brutus', to Cassius'; burn all. Some to Decius' house, and
some to Casca's, some to Ligarius'. Away, go!

[Exeunt.]

FIRST CITIZEN: *As a friend or an enemy?*

CINNA: *As a friend.*

SECOND CITIZEN: *That matter is answered directly.*

FOURTH CITIZEN: *Where do you live—briefly.*

CINNA: *Briefly, I live near the Capitol.*

THIRD CITIZEN: *Your name, sir, truly.*

CINNA: *Truly, my name is Cinna.*

FIRST CITIZEN: *Kill him. Tear him to pieces; he's a conspirator.*

CINNA: *I am Cinna the poet; I am Cinna the poet.*

FOURTH CITIZEN: *Kill him for his bad poetry; kill him for his bad poetry.*

CINNA: *I am not Cinna the conspirator.*

FOURTH CITIZEN: *It doesn't matter; his name's Cinna. Let us rip his name out of his heart and send him packing.*

THIRD CITIZEN: *Kill him! Kill him! Come, torches here! Firebrands to Brutus', to Cassius'. Burn all their homes. Some of you go to Decius' house, and some to Casca's, some to Ligarius'. Away. Go!* [Exit.]

ACT IV

SCENE 1
A house in Rome.

[Antony, Octavius, and Lepidus, seated at a table.]

ANTONY: These many then shall die, their names are prick'd.

OCTAVIUS: Your brother too must die; consent you, Lepidus?

LEPIDUS: I do consent—

OCTAVIUS: Prick him down, Antony.

5   LEPIDUS: Upon condition Publius shall not live,
        Who is your sister's son, Mark Antony.

ANTONY: He shall not live; look, with a spot I damn him.
        But, Lepidus, go you to Caesar's house,
        Fetch the will hither, and we shall determine
10   How to cut off some charge in legacies.

LEPIDUS: What, shall I find you here?

OCTAVIUS: Or here, or at the Capitol.   *[Exit Lepidus.]*

ANTONY: This is a slight unmeritable man,
        Meet to be sent on errands. Is it fit,
15   The three-fold world divided, he should stand
        One of the three to share it?

ACT IV

SCENE 1
A house in Rome.

[Antony, Octavius, and Lepidus, seated at a table.]

ANTONY: *Then, these shall all die; their names are marked here.*

OCTAVIUS: *Your brother too must die. Do you consent, Lepidus?*

LEPIDUS: *I give my consent—*

OCTAVIUS: *Mark him down, Antony.*

LEPIDUS: *On the condition Publius, who is your sister's son, shall not live either, Mark Antony.*

ANTONY: *He shall not live. Look, with a mark I damn him. But, Lepidus, go to Caesar's house and bring his will here. We will determine how to alter some charge in legacies of the people.*

LEPIDUS: *Shall I return to you here?*

OCTAVIUS: *Here, or at the Capitol.*   [Exit Lepidus.]

ANTONY: *He is a slight, unworthy man, fit only to be sent on errands. Should he stand to share one third of the world which we will divide?*

OCTAVIUS: So you thought him,
    And took his voice who should be prick'd to die
    In our black sentence and proscription.

20   ANTONY: Octavius, I have seen more days than you,
    And though we lay these honors on this man
    To ease ourselves of divers slanderous loads,
    He shall but bear them as the ass bears gold,
    To groan and sweat under the business,
25   Either led or driven, as we point the way;
    And having brought our treasure where we will,
    Then take we down his load and turn him off,
    Like to the empty ass, to shake his ears
    And graze in commons.

30   OCTAVIUS: You may do your will,
    But he's a tried and valiant soldier.

    ANTONY: So is my horse, Octavius, and for that
    I do appoint him store of provender.
    It is a creature that I teach to fight,
35   To wind, to stop, to run directly on,
    His corporal motion govern'd by my spirit.
    And, in some taste, is Lepidus but so:
    He must be taught, and train'd, and bid go forth;
    A barren-spirited fellow, one that feeds
40   On abjects, orts, and imitations,
    Which, out of use and staled by other men,
    Begin his fashion. Do not talk of him
    But as a property. And now, Octavius,
    Listen great things. Brutus and Cassius
45   Are levying powers; we must straight make head;
    Therefore let our alliance be combined,
    Our best friends made, our means stretch'd;
    And let us presently go sit in council,
    How covert matters may be best disclosed,
50   And open perils surest answered.

OCTAVIUS: *You thought him worthy, and you listened to his advice as to whom on our list would be executed.*

ANTONY: *Octavius, I am older than you. Although we lay these honors upon this man to rid ourselves of some of the blame for these deaths, he shall bear them only as the ass bears gold. He will groan and sweat under the business and be led or driven as we desire. And having brought our treasure where we want, we will lighten his load and let him go to return to common ways like a jackass shaking his head.*

OCTAVIUS: *You may do what you want, but remember he's a tried and valiant soldier.*

ANTONY: *So is my horse, Octavius, but I give him only food and shelter for all that. It is an animal that I teach to fight, to turn, to stop, to run directly on, his motions governed by my spirit. Lepidus is like that. He must be taught and trained and told where to go. He is a dull man, one who feeds on trivial things which are not even fashionable any longer. Do not talk of him, except as an object. And now, Octavius, listen to great things. Brutus and Cassius are raising armies. We must act immediately. Therefore, let our alliance be strengthened, our best friends made, our advantages extended. Let us presently go sit in council, and discuss how to discover hidden problems and dangers.*

OCTAVIUS: Let us do so, for we are at the stake,
    And bay'd about with many enemies;
    And some that smile have in their hearts, I fear,
    Millions of mischiefs.   *[Exeunt.]*

SCENE 2
Camp near Sardis.
Before Brutus' tent. Drum.

[Enter Brutus, Lucilius, Lucius, and Soldiers; Titinius and Pindarus meet them.]

BRUTUS: Stand, ho!

LUCILIUS: Give the word, ho, and stand.

BRUTUS: What now, Lucilius, is Cassius near?

LUCILIUS: He is at hand, and Pindarus is come
5   To do you salutation from his master.

BRUTUS: He greets me well. Your master, Pindarus,
    In his own change, or by ill officers,
    Hath given me some worthy cause to wish
    Things done undone; but if he be at hand,
10   I shall be satisfied.

PINDARUS: I do not doubt
    But that my noble master will appear
    Such as he is, full of regard and honor.

BRUTUS: He is not doubted. A word, Lucilius,
15   How he received you. Let me be resolved.

OCTAVIUS: *Let us do so. We are tied to a stake and barked at by many ene-mies, some of whose smiles mask evil motives.*

[Exit.]

SCENE 2
Camp near Sardis.
Before Brutus' tent. Drum.

[Enter Brutus, Lucilius, Lucius, and Soldiers; Titinius and Pindarus meet them.]

BRUTUS: *Stand, ready!*

LUCILIUS: *Give the word, now, and stand.*

BRUTUS: *What is it, Lucilius? Is Cassius near by?*

LUCILIUS: *He is at hand, and Pindarus has come to give you greetings from his master.*

BRUTUS: [To Pindarus.] *He honors me well. Your master, Pindarus, either by his own thinking or by persuasion of his officers, has given me a valid reason to wish things already done could be undone. But, if he is near-by, I will be satisfied by him personally.*

PINDARUS: *I know that my noble master will appear and give you satisfac-tion and honor.*

BRUTUS: *I do not doubt him.* [Aside to Lucilius.] *A word, Lucilius. How has he received you? Let me know how Cassius treated you.*

139

LUCILIUS: With courtesy and with respect enough,
 But not with such familiar instances,
 Nor with such free and friendly conference,
 As he hath used of old.

20 BRUTUS: Thou hast described
 A hot friend cooling. Ever note, Lucilius,
 When love begins to sicken and decay
 It useth an enforced ceremony.
 There are no tricks in plain and simple faith;
25 But hollow men, like horses hot at hand,
 Make gallant show and promise of their mettle;
 But when they should endure the bloody spur,
 They fall their crests and like deceitful jades
 Sink in the trial. Comes his army on?

30 LUCILIUS: They mean his night in Sardis to be quarter'd;
 The greater part, the horse in general,
 Are come with Cassius.   *[Low march within.]*

 BRUTUS: Hark, he is arrived.
 March gently on to meet him.

[Enter Cassius and his powers.]

35 CASSIUS: Stand, ho!

 BRUTUS: Stand, ho! Speak the word along.

 FIRST SOLDIER: Stand!

 SECOND SOLDIER: Stand!

 THIRD SOLDIER: Stand!

40 CASSIUS: Most noble brother, you have done me wrong.

140

LUCILIUS: *Surely with courtesy and with enough respect. However, not with the intimacies and talk you would expect from an old friend.*

BRUTUS: *You have described a hot friend cooling. Lucilius, note how forced the ceremony becomes when friendship is withering. There are no tricks in plain and simple faith. But, hollow men, like fiery horses, make gallant show and promise of their prowess; but when they should back up their words, they fail to do so. Does his army come?*

LUCILIUS: *They mean to be quartered this night in Sardis; the larger part, his cavalry, has come with Cassius.*   [Low march within.]

BRUTUS: *Listen! He has arrived. March gently on to meet him.*

[Enter Cassius and others.]

CASSIUS: *Stand, ready!*

BRUTUS: *Stand, ready! Spread the word.*

FIRST SOLDIER: *Stand!*

SECOND SOLDIER: *Stand!*

THIRD SOLDIER: *Stand!*

CASSIUS: *Most noble brother, you have done me wrong.*

BRUTUS: Judge me, you gods! Wrong I mine enemies?
    And, if not so, how should I wrong a brother?

CASSIUS: Brutus, this sober form of yours hides wrongs,
    And when you do them—

45 BRUTUS: Cassius, be content,
    Speak your griefs softly, I do know you well.
    Before the eyes of both our armies here,
    Which should perceive nothing but love from us,
    Let us not wrangle. Bid them move away;
50   Then in my tent, Cassius, enlarge your griefs,
    And I will give you audience.

CASSIUS: Pindarus,
    Bid our commanders lead their charges off
    A little from this ground.

55 BRUTUS: Lucilius, do you the like, and let no man
    Come to our tent till we have done our conference.
    Let Lucius and Titinius guard our door.   *[Exeunt.]*

BRUTUS: *Judge me, you gods! Do I wrong even my enemies? If not, how should I wrong a brother?*

CASSIUS: *Brutus, this sober face of yours masks wrongs; and when you do them—*

BRUTUS: *Cassius, be content. Speak your concerns softly; we should not quarrel in front of our two armies who should see us only friendly. Have your men moved away; then in my tent, Cassius, you may spread your complaints and I will listen to you.*

CASSIUS: *Pindarus, bid our commanders lead their men away from this ground.*

BRUTUS: *Lucilius, you do the same. Let no man come to our tent until we have finished our conference. Let Lucius and Titinius guard our door.*
                                                    [Exit.]

SCENE 3
Brutus' tent.

[Enter Brutus and Cassius.]

CASSIUS: That you have wrong'd me doth appear in this:
    You have condemn'd and noted Lucius Pella
    For taking bribes here of the Sardians,
    Wherein my letters, praying on his side,
5   Because I knew the man, were slighted off.

BRUTUS: You wrong'd yourself to write in such a case.

CASSIUS: In such a time as this it is not meet
    That every nice offense should bear his comment.

BRUTUS: Let me tell you, Cassius, you yourself
10   Are much condemn'd to have an itching palm,
    To sell and mart your offices for gold
    To undeservers.

CASSIUS: I an itching palm?
    You know that you are Brutus that speaks this,
15   Or, by the gods, this speech were else your last.

BRUTUS: The name of Cassius honors this corruption,
    And chastisement doth therefore hide his head.

CASSIUS: Chastisement?

BRUTUS: Remember March, the ides of March remember.
20   Did not great Julius bleed for justice' sake?
    What villain touch'd his body, that did stab,
    And not for justice? What, shall one of us,
    That struck the foremost man of all this world
    But for supporting robbers, shall we now
25   Contaminate our fingers with base bribes

SCENE 3
Brutus' tent.

[Enter Brutus and Cassius.]

CASSIUS: *I believe you have intentionally wronged me. You have condemned and disgraced Lucius Pella for taking bribes here of the Sardians. My letters on his behalf were disregarded.*

BRUTUS: *You wronged yourself to write in such a case.*

CASSIUS: *In such a time as this it is not good that every small offense should be scrutinized.*

BRUTUS: *Let me tell you, Cassius, you yourself are much condemned to have a greediness for taking bribes and selling your offices for gold to those who don't deserve it.*

CASSIUS: *I take bribes! By the gods, if it were not Brutus who spoke, this speech would be your last.*

BRUTUS: *Because the name of Cassius is connected to this corruption, punishment is not possible.*

CASSIUS: *Punishment!*

BRUTUS: *Remember March—the ides of March—remember. Did not great Julius bleed for justice's sake? Which of us stabbed him except to get justice? Shall one of us, who struck the foremost man of all this world, do it only to support robbers? Shall we now contaminate our fingers with base bribes and sell the mighty space of our large honors for so much trash as we might grasp? I would rather be a dog and bay at the moon than be such a Roman.*

And sell the mighty space of our large honors
For so much trash as may be grasped thus?
I had rather be a dog, and bay the moon,
Than such a Roman.

30   CASSIUS: Brutus, bait not me,
I'll not endure it. You forget yourself
To hedge me in. I am a soldier, I,
Older in practice, abler than yourself
To make conditions.

35   BRUTUS: Go to, you are not, Cassius.

CASSIUS: I am.

BRUTUS: I say you are not.

CASSIUS: Urge me no more, I shall forget myself;
Have mind upon your health, tempt me no farther.

40   BRUTUS: Away, slight man!

CASSIUS: Is't possible?

BRUTUS: Hear me, for I will speak.
Must I give way and room to your rash choler?
Shall I be frighted when a madman stares?

45   CASSIUS: O gods, ye gods! Must I endure all this?

BRUTUS: All this? Ay, more. Fret till your proud heart break.
Go show your slaves how choleric you are,
And make your bondmen tremble. Must I bouge?
Must I observe you? Must I stand and crouch
50   Under your testy humor? By the gods,
You shall digest the venom of your spleen,
Though it do split you, for, from this day forth,
I'll use you for my mirth, yea, for my laughter,
When you are waspish.

CASSIUS: *Brutus, do not bark at me; I will not endure it. You forget yourself when you try to restrict me. I am a soldier. I am older in practice and abler than you to manage things.*

BRUTUS: *Enough! you are not, Cassius.*

CASSIUS: *I am.*

BRUTUS: *I say you are not.*

CASSIUS: *Urge me no more, or I will forget myself. Be mindful of your health; tempt me no farther.*

BRUTUS: *Away, slight man!*

CASSIUS: *Is it possible?*

BRUTUS: *Hear me, for I will speak. Must I give way and room to your rash anger? Will I be frighted when a madman stares?*

CASSIUS: *Oh, gods, gods! Must I endure all this?*

BRUTUS: *All this? Yes, and more. Worry until your proud heart breaks. Go show your slaves how angry you are, and make your slaves tremble. Must I budge? Must I observe you? Must I stand and crouch under your testy attitude? By the gods, you shall digest the poison of your own temper even if it split you apart. For, from this day on, I'll use you for my humor; yes, for my own laughter, when you are angry.*

CASSIUS: Is it come to this?

55   BRUTUS: You say you are a better soldier:
         Let it appear so, make your vaunting true,
         And it shall please me well. For mine own part,
         I shall be glad to learn of noble men.

     CASSIUS: You wrong me every way, you wrong me, Brutus.
60   I said, an elder soldier, not a better.
         Did I say "better"?

     BRUTUS: If you did, I care not.

     CASSIUS: When Caesar lived, he durst not thus have moved me.

     BRUTUS: Peace, peace! You durst not so have tempted him.

65   CASSIUS: I durst not?

     BRUTUS: No.

     CASSIUS: What, durst not tempt him?

     BRUTUS: For your life you durst not.

     CASSIUS: Do not presume too much upon my love;
70   I may do that I shall be sorry for.

     BRUTUS: You have done that you should be sorry for.
         There is no terror, Cassius, in your threats,
         For I am arm'd so strong in honesty,
         That they pass by me as the idle wind
75   Which I respect not. I did send to you
         For certain sums of gold, which you denied me,
         For I can raise no money by vile means.
         By heaven, I had rather coin my heart
         And drop my blood for drachmas than to wring
80   From the hard hands of peasants their vile trash

148

CASSIUS: Has it come to this?

BRUTUS: You say you are a better soldier; maybe it is so. Make your bragging true, and it will please me well. For my own part, I shall be glad to learn from noble men.

CASSIUS: You wrong me every way; you wrong me, Brutus. I said an older soldier not a better one. Did I say "better"?

BRUTUS: If you did, I don't care.

CASSIUS: When Caesar lived, he could not have moved me like this.

BRUTUS: Peace, peace! You dared not tempt him like this.

CASSIUS: I didn't?

BRUTUS: No.

CASSIUS: What, you mean I did not dare to tempt him?

BRUTUS: For your life you didn't.

CASSIUS: Do not presume too much upon my loyalty; I may do that which I shall be sorry for later.

BRUTUS: You have done something that you should be sorry for. There is no teeth, Cassius, in your threats; for I am armed so strong in honesty that threats pass me by as the idle wind does. I sent to you for certain sums of gold which you denied me. I can raise no money by wicked means. I would rather raise coin from my heart and blood rather than dishonestly wring them from poor peasants by lies. I asked you for gold to pay my legions, which you denied me. Was that done like Cassius? Should I have answered Caius Cassius so? When Marcus Brutus grows so greedy as to lock such worthless pieces from his friends, be ready, gods, with all your thunderbolts—to dash him to pieces!

By any indirection. I did send
To you for gold to pay my legions,
Which you denied me. Was that done like Cassius?
Should I have answer'd Caius Cassius so?
85   When Marcus Brutus grows so covetous
To lock such rascal counters from his friends,
Be ready, gods, with all your thunderbolts,
Dash him to pieces!

CASSIUS: I denied you not.

90   BRUTUS: You did.

CASSIUS: I did not. He was but a fool
That brought my answer back. Brutus hath rived my heart.
A friend should bear his friend's infirmities,
But Brutus makes mine greater than they are.

95   BRUTUS: I do not, till you practise them on me.

CASSIUS: You love me not.

BRUTUS: I do not like your faults.

CASSIUS: A friendly eye could never see such faults.

BRUTUS: A flatterer's would not, though they do appear
100   As huge as high Olympus.

CASSIUS: Come, Antony, and young Octavius, come,
Revenge yourselves alone on Cassius,
For Cassius is aweary of the world:
Hated by one he loves; braved by his brother;
105   Check'd like a bondman; all his faults observed,
Set in a notebook, learn'd and conn'd by rote,
To cast into my teeth. O, I could weep
My spirit from mine eyes! There is my dagger,
And here my naked breast; within, a heart

CASSIUS: *I denied you nothing.*

BRUTUS: *You did.*

CASSIUS: *I did not. He that brought my answer back was only a fool. Brutus has torn my heart. A friend should bear his friend's weaknesses, but Brutus makes mine greater than they are.*

BRUTUS: *I did not until you tried them on me.*

CASSIUS: *You do not like me.*

BRUTUS: *I do not like your faults.*

CASSIUS: *A friendly eye would never see such faults.*

BRUTUS: *A flatterer's eye would not, though they appear as huge as high Olympus.*

CASSIUS: *Come, Antony, and young Octavius, come. Revenge yourselves on Cassius, for Cassius is weary of this world—hated by one he loves, defied by his brother, talked to like a slave. All of my faults are observed, noted, learned, and memorized to be thrown into my teeth. I could weep my spirit from my eyes! There is my dagger, and here my naked breast; within lies a heart dearer than Pluto's, richer than gold. If you are really a Roman, pluck it out. I, who denied you gold, will give you my heart. Strike as you did at Caesar. I know that, even when you hated him worst, you loved him better than ever you loved Cassius.*

110   Dearer than Pluto's mine, richer than gold.
        If that thou best a Roman, take it forth;
        I, that denied thee gold, will give my heart.
        Strike, as thou didst at Caesar, for I know,
        When thou didst hate him worst, thou lovedst him better
115   Than ever thou lovedst Cassius.

        BRUTUS: Sheathe your dagger.
        Be angry when you will, it shall have scope;
        Do what you will, dishonor shall be humor.
        O Cassius, you are yoked with a lamb,
120   That carries anger as the flint bears fire,
        Who, much enforced, shows a hasty spark
        And straight is cold again.

        CASSIUS: Hath Cassius lived
        To be but mirth and laughter to his Brutus,
125   When grief and blood ill-temper'd vexeth him?

        BRUTUS: When I spoke that, I was ill-temper'd too.

        CASSIUS: Do you confess so much? Give me your hand.

        BRUTUS: And my heart too.

        CASSIUS: O Brutus!

130   BRUTUS: What's the matter?

        CASSIUS: Have not you love enough to bear with me,
        When that rash humor which my mother gave me
        Makes me forgetful?

        BRUTUS: Yes, Cassius, and from henceforth,
135   When you are overearnest with your Brutus,
        He'll think your mother chides, and leave you so.

BRUTUS: *Put away your dagger. Be angry when you will; your anger will have its freedom. Do whatever you will, the insults are prompted by anger. Cassius, you are tied to a lamb that carries anger as the flint holds fire; when struck, an angry spark flares, but immediately after grows cold again.*

CASSIUS: *Has Cassius lived to be only humorous to his Brutus when griefs trouble him?*

BRUTUS: *When I spoke that, I was troubled too.*

CASSIUS: *Do you confess so much? Give me your hand.*

BRUTUS: *And my heart, too.*

CASSIUS: *Oh, Brutus!*

BRUTUS: *What's the matter?*

CASSIUS: *Do you care enough for me to put up with this rashness which I've inherited from my mother?*

BRUTUS: *Yes, Cassius. From now on, when you are too intense with your Brutus, he'll think your mother jokes—and I'll leave you so.*

POET: *[Within.]* Let me go in to see the generals.
There is some grudge between 'em, 'tis not meet
They be alone.

140   LUCILIUS: *[Within.]* You shall not come to them.

POET: *[Within.]* Nothing but death shall stay me.

[Enter Poet, followed by Lucilius, Titinius, and Lucius.]

CASSIUS: How now, what's the matter?

POET: For shame, you generals! What do you mean?
Love, and be friends, as two such men should be;
145   For I have seen more years, I'm sure, than ye.

CASSIUS: Ha, ha! How vilely doth this cynic rhyme!

BRUTUS: Get you hence, sirrah; saucy fellow, hence!

CASSIUS: Bear with him, Brutus; 'tis his fashion.

BRUTUS: I'll know his humor when he knows his time.
150   What should the wars do with these jigging fools?
Companion, hence!

CASSIUS: Away, away, be gone!   *[Exit Poet.]*

BRUTUS: Lucilius and Titinius, bid the commanders
Prepare to lodge their companies tonight.

155   CASSIUS: And come yourselves and bring Messala with you
Immediately to us.   *[Exeunt Lucilius and Titinius.]*

BRUTUS: Lucius, a bowl of wine!   *[Exit Lucius.]*

CASSIUS: I did not think you could have been so angry.

154

POET: [Within.] *Let me go in to see the generals; there is some grudge between them. It is not good that they are alone.*

LUCILIUS: [Within.] *You shall not come to them.*

POET: [Within.] *Nothing but death will stop me.*

[Enter Poet, followed by Lucilius, Titinius, and Lucius.]

CASSIUS: Well! What's the matter?

POET: *For shame, you generals! What do you mean? Be friends, as two such men should be; for I have seen many more years than you, I'm sure.*

CASSIUS: Ha, ha! How poorly does this rude poet rhyme!

BRUTUS: Get away, sir; silly man, away!

CASSIUS: Put up with him, Brutus; it is his fashion.

BRUTUS: *I'll tolerate him when he knows a better time to come. What do wars have to do with these jigging fools? Man, away!*

CASSIUS: Away. Away. Be gone!   [Exit Poet.]

BRUTUS: *Lucilius and Titinius. Bid the commanders to prepare to camp their companies here tonight.*

CASSIUS: *Bring Messala and yourself immediately to us.*
                                    [Exit Lucilius and Titinius.]

BRUTUS: Lucius, a bowl of wine! [Exit Lucius.]

CASSIUS: *I did not think you could have been so angry.*

BRUTUS: O Cassius, I am sick of many griefs.

160 CASSIUS: Of your philosophy you make no use,
    If you give place to accidental evils.

BRUTUS: No man bears sorrow better. Portia is dead.

CASSIUS: Ha? Portia?

BRUTUS: She is dead.

165 CASSIUS: How 'scaped killing when I cross'd you so?
    O insupportable and touching loss!
    Upon what sickness?

BRUTUS: Impatient of my absence,
    And grief that young Octavius with Mark Antony
175   Have made themselves so strong: for with her death
    That tidings came: with this she fell distract,
    And, her attendants absent, swallow'd fire.

CASSIUS: And died so?

BRUTUS: Even so.

180 CASSIUS: O ye immortal gods!

[Re-enter Lucius, with wine and taper.]

185 BRUTUS: Speak no more of her. Give me a bowl of wine.
    In this I bury all unkindness, Cassius.   *[Drinks.]*

CASSIUS: My heart is thirsty for that noble pledge.
    Fill, Lucius, till the wine o'erswell the cup;
    I cannot drink too much of Brutus' love.   *[Drinks.]*

190 BRUTUS: Come in, Titinius!   *[Exit Lucius.]*

BRUTUS: *Oh, Cassius, I am tired of many concerns.*

CASSIUS: *You make no use of your philosophy; you are affected by chance.*

BRUTUS: *No man bears sorrow better. Portia is dead.*

CASSIUS: *What! Portia?*

BRUTUS: *She is dead.*

CASSIUS: *How did I escape dying when I irritated you so? Oh, huge and touching loss! What did she die of?*

BRUTUS: *I've been told that impatient at my absence and grieving that young Octavius and Mark Antony had made themselves so very strong—she became depressed and swallowed burning coals.*

CASSIUS: *And so she died?*

BRUTUS: *Even so.*

CASSIUS: *Oh, you immortal gods!*

[Re-enter Lucius, with wine and taper.]

BRUTUS: *Speak no more of her. Give me a bowl of wine. In this I will bury all sorrow, Cassius.*   [Drinks.]

CASSIUS: *My heart is thirsty for that noble pledge. Fill, Lucius, until the wine laps over the cup; I cannot drink too much of Brutus' love.*
                                        [Drinks.]

BRUTUS: *Come in, Titinius!*   [Exit Lucius.]

[Re-enter Titinius, with Messala.]
                    Welcome, good Messala.
Now sit we close about this taper here,
And call in question our necessities.

CASSIUS: Portia, art thou gone?

195 BRUTUS: No more, I pray you.
Messala, I have here received letters
That young Octavius and Mark Antony
Come down upon us with a mighty power,
Bending their expedition toward Philippi.

200 MESSALA: Myself have letters of the selfsame tenure.

BRUTUS: With what addition?

MESSALA: That by proscription and bills of outlawry
Octavius, Antony, and Lepidus
Have put to death an hundred senators.

205 BRUTUS: Therein our letters do not well agree;
Mine speak of seventy senators that died
By their proscriptions, Cicero being one.

CASSIUS: Cicero one!

MESSALA: Cicero is dead,
210 And by that order of proscription.
Had you your letters from your wife, my lord?

BRUTUS: No, Messala.

MESSALA: Nor nothing in your letters writ of her?

BRUTUS: Nothing, Messala.

215 MESSALA: That, methinks, is strange.

[Re-enter Titinius, with Messala.]

Welcome, good Messala. Sit close around this candle here, and let us discuss our plan.

CASSIUS: *Portia, are you really gone?*

BRUTUS: *No more of this, I pray you. Messala, I have received letters detailing that young Octavius and Mark Antony come down upon us with a mighty power, marching their forces towards Philippi.*

MESSALA: *I myself have letters of the selfsame tune.*

BRUTUS: *With what additions?*

MESSALA: *Only that by enacting new proclamations, Octavius, Antony, and Lepidus have put to death a hundred senators.*

BRUTUS: *Our letters do not agree. Mine speak of seventy senators who died by their proscriptions, Cicero being one.*

CASSIUS: *Cicero!*

MESSALA: *Cicero is dead, and by that very order. Have you had any letters from your wife, my lord?*

BRUTUS: *No, Messala.*

MESSALA: *Nor received nothing in your letters written about her?*

BRUTUS: *Nothing, Messala.*

MESSALA: *That, I think, is strange.*

BRUTUS: Why ask you? Hear you ought of her in yours?

MESSALA: No, my lord.

BRUTUS: Now, as you are a Roman, tell me true.

MESSALA: Then like a Roman bear the truth I tell:
220   For certain she is dead, and by strange manner.

BRUTUS: Why, farewell, Portia. We must die, Messala.
    With meditating that she must die once
    I have the patience to endure it now.

MESSALA: Even so great men great losses should endure.

225 CASSIUS: I have as much of this in art as you,
    But yet my nature could not bear it so.

BRUTUS: Well, to our work alive. What do you think
    Of marching to Philippi presently?

CASSIUS: I do not think it good.

230 BRUTUS: Your reason?

CASSIUS: This it is:
    'Tis better that the enemy seek us;
    So shall he waste his means, weary his soldiers,
    Doing himself offense, whilst we lying still
235   Are full of rest, defense, and nimbleness.

BRUTUS: Good reasons must of force give place to better.
    The people 'twixt Philippi and this ground
    Do stand but in a forced affection,
    For they have grudged us contribution.
240   The enemy, marching along by them,
    By them shall make a fuller number up,
    Come on refresh'd, new-added, and encouraged;

BRUTUS: *Why do you ask? Do you hear of her in yours?*

MESSALA: *No, my lord.*

BRUTUS: *Now, as you are a Roman, tell me the truth.*

MESSALA: *Then like a Roman, bear the truth I tell—for certainly she is dead, and by strange means.*

BRUTUS: *Why, farewell, Portia. We all must die, Messala. By meditating on her death, I have the will to endure it now.*

MESSALA: *Even great men must endure great losses.*

CASSIUS: *I have as much patience and endurance as you, but my nature could not bear it as you do.*

BRUTUS: *Well, we must turn to our work. What do you think of marching to Philippi immediately?*

CASSIUS: *I do not think it wise.*

BRUTUS: *Your reason?*

CASSIUS: *Here it is. It is better that the enemy seek us. We shall waste his means, weary his soldiers, do him offense. We, on the other hand, will be full of rest, defense, and energy.*

BRUTUS: *Good reasons must, of course, give way to better ones. The people between Philippi and our position are with us only because of the forces here. They have given us contributions only grudgingly. The enemy, by marching along near them, will add fuller numbers, come on refreshed, larger, and encouraged. We shall cut him off from this advantage if we do face him there, at Philippi, with these people at our back.*

From which advantage shall we cut him off
If at Philippi we do face him there,
245   These people at our back.

CASSIUS: Hear me, good brother.

BRUTUS: Under your pardon. You must note beside
That we have tried the utmost of our friends,
Our legions are brim-full, our cause is ripe:
250   The enemy increaseth every day;
We, at the height, are ready to decline.
There is a tide in the affairs of men
Which taken at the flood leads on to fortune;
Omitted, all the voyage of their life
255   Is bound in shallows and in miseries.
On such a full sea are we now afloat,
And we must take the current when it serves,
Or lose our ventures.

CASSIUS: Then, with your will, go on;
260   We'll along ourselves and meet them at Philippi.

BRUTUS: The deep of night is crept upon our talk,
And nature must obey necessity,
Which we will niggard with a little rest.
There is no more to say?

265   CASSIUS: No more. Good night.
Early tomorrow will we rise and hence.

BRUTUS: Lucius! *[Re-enter Lucius.]* My gown.   *[Exit Lucius.]*
Farewell, good Messala;
Good night, Titinius; noble, noble Cassius,
270   Good night and good repose.

CASSIUS: O my dear brother!
This was an ill beginning of the night.
Never come such division 'tween our souls!
Let it not, Brutus.

CASSIUS: *Hear me, good brother.*

BRUTUS: *I beg your pardon. You must note besides that we have added as many soldiers as we can expect ever to have—our legions are brim-full, our cause is ripe, and the enemy increases every day. We, however, are ready to decline from this height. There is a time in the affairs of men in which it is the precisely right moment to act. If this moment to launch a course of action is not grasped, all the voyages of their lives will be bound in shallows and in miseries. On such a full sea are we now afloat, and we must take the current when it is the right time or risk losing our ventures.*

CASSIUS: *Then, with your will, go on. We'll come along ourselves and meet them at Philippi.*

BRUTUS: *The night has crept upon our discussion, and nature must obey necessity. We will need a little rest. Is there no more to say?*

CASSIUS: *No more. Good night. Early tomorrow will we rise and leave for Philippi.*

BRUTUS: *Lucius!* [Re-enter Lucius.] *My gown.*
                                         [Exit Lucius.]
Farewell, good Messala. Good night, Titinius; noble, noble Cassius, good night and sleep well.

CASSIUS: *My dear brother! This was an ill beginning to this night. Never has such division come between our souls! Let it not stay there, Brutus.*

275 BRUTUS: Every thing is well.

CASSIUS: Good night, my lord.

BRUTUS: Good night, good brother.

TITINIUS AND MESSALA: Good night, Lord Brutus.

BRUTUS: Farewell, everyone.

[Exeunt all but Brutus.]

[Re-enter Lucius, with the gown.]
280   Give me the gown. Where is thy instrument?

LUCIUS: Here in the tent.

BRUTUS: What, thou speak'st drowsily?
    Poor knave, I blame thee not, thou art o'erwatch'd.
    Call Claudius and some other of my men,
285   I'll have them sleep on cushions in my tent.

LUCIUS: Varro and Claudio!

[Enter Varro and Claudio.]

VARRO: Calls my lord?

BRUTUS: I pray you, sirs, lie in my tent and sleep;
    It may be I shall raise you by and by
290   On business to my brother Cassius.

VARRO: So please you, we will stand and watch your pleasure.

BRUTUS: I will not have it so. Lie down, good sirs.
    It may be I shall otherwise bethink me.
    Look, Lucius, here's the book I sought for so;
295   I put it in the pocket of my gown.

[Varro and Claudio lie down.]

164

BRUTUS: *Everything is well.*

CASSIUS: *Good night, my lord.*

BRUTUS: *Good night, good brother.*

TITINIUS AND MESSALA: *Good night, Lord Brutus.*

BRUTUS: *Farewell, everyone.*
[Exit all but Brutus.]

[Re-enter Lucius, with the gown.]
Give me the gown. Where is your musical instrument?

LUCIUS: *Here in the tent.*

BRUTUS: *What? You speak in a sleepy way. Poor boy, I don't blame you; you have stayed up all night waiting. Call Claudius and some other of my men. I'll have them in my tent.*

LUCIUS: *Varro and Claudius!*

[Enter Varro and Claudius.]

VARRO: *Does my lord call?*

BRUTUS: *I ask you, sir, come join me in my tent and sleep. It may chance that I shall need to send you to my brother Cassius on business.*

VARRO: *Certainly, sir. We will stand and wait on your wishes.*

BRUTUS: *I would not have it so. Please lie down, good sirs. I may yet change my mind about the messages. Look, Lucius; here's the book I sent you for. I put it in the pocket of my gown.* [Varro and Claudius lie down.]

LUCIUS: I was sure your lordship did not give it me.

BRUTUS: Bear with me, good boy, I am much forgetful.
 Canst thou hold up thy heavy eyes a while,
 And touch thy instrument a strain or two?

300 LUCIUS: Ay, my lord, an't please you.

BRUTUS: It does, my boy.
 I trouble thee too much, but thou art willing.

LUCIUS: It is my duty, sir.

BRUTUS: I should not urge thy duty past thy might;
305 I know young bloods look for a time of rest.

LUCIUS: I have slept, my lord, already.

BRUTUS: It was well done, and thou shalt sleep again;
 I will not hold thee long. If I do live,
 I will be good to thee.   *[Music, and a song.]*
310 This is a sleepy tune. O murderous slumber,
 Layest thou thy leaden mace upon my boy
 That plays thee music? Gentle knave, good night.
 I will not do thee so much wrong to wake thee.
 If thou dost nod, thou break'st thy instrument;
315 I'll take it from thee; and, good boy, good night.
 Let me see, let me see; is not the leaf turn'd down
 Where I left reading? Here it is, I think. *[Sits down.]*

[Enter the Ghost of Caesar.]
 How ill this taper burns! Ha, who comes here?
 I think it is the weakness of mine eyes
320 That shapes this monstrous apparition.
 It comes upon me. Art thou any thing?
 Art thou some god, some angel, or some devil
 That makest my blood cold, and my hair to stare?
 Speak to me what thou art.

166

LUCIUS: *I was sure your lordship did not give it to me.*

BRUTUS: *Bear with me, good boy; I am very forgetful. Could you hold up your heavy eyelids awhile, and play a tune or two for me?*

LUCIUS: *Yes, my lord, if it would please you.*

BRUTUS: *It does, my boy. I know I trouble you, but you are willing.*

LUCIUS: *It is my duty, sir.*

BRUTUS: *I should not urge your duty past your will; I know young bloods need a time of rest.*

LUCIUS: *I have slept, my lord, already.*

BRUTUS: *It was done well, and you shall sleep again soon. I will not hold you long. If I do live, I will be good to you.* [Music, and a song.]
This is a sleepy tune. [As Brutus and Lucius nod off, Brutus notices Lucius has fallen asleep.] *Oh, murderous slumber, do you lay your leaden weapon upon my boy who plays you music? Gentle boy, good night; I will not wake you. As you do nod, you'll break your instrument. I'll take it from you. Good boy, good night. Let me see; let me see. Have I not turned a corner on the book I was reading? Here it is, I think.*
[Sits down.]

[After a moment enter the Ghost of Caesar.]
How ill this candle burns! Ah! Who comes here? I think it is the weakness of my eyes that shapes this monstrous ghost. It comes upon me. Are you real? Are you some god, some angel, or some devil that makes my blood cold and my hair stand on end? Speak to me—what are you?

167

325   GHOST: Thy evil spirit, Brutus.

     BRUTUS: Why comest thou?

     GHOST: To tell thee thou shalt see me at Philippi.

     BRUTUS: Well, then I shall see thee again?

     GHOST: Ay, at Philippi.

330   BRUTUS: Why, I will see thee at Philippi then.

                                         [Exit Ghost.]
       Now I have taken heart thou vanishest.
       Ill spirit, I would hold more talk with thee.
       Boy, Lucius! Varro! Claudius! Sirs, awake!
       Claudius!

335   LUCIUS: The strings, my lord, are false.

     BRUTUS: He thinks he still is at his instrument.
       Lucius, awake!

     LUCIUS: My lord?

     BRUTUS: Didst thou dream, Lucius, that thou so criedst out?

340   LUCIUS: My lord, I do not know that I did cry.

     BRUTUS: Yes, that thou didst. Didst thou see any thing?

     LUCIUS: Nothing, my lord.

     BRUTUS: Sleep again, Lucius. Sirrah Claudius!
       [To Varro.] Fellow thou, awake!

345   VARRO: My lord?

     CLAUDIUS: My lord?

GHOST: *Your evil spirit, Brutus.*

BRUTUS: *Why did you come here?*

GHOST: *To tell you that you will see me at Philippi.*

BRUTUS: *What, I'll see you again?*

GHOST: *Yes, at Philippi.*

BRUTUS: *Why, I will see you at Philippi then.*   [Exit Ghost.]
I can now take heart since the ghost has vanished. Ill spirit, I wish to hold more talk with you. Boy! Lucius! Varro! Claudius! Sirs, awake! Claudius!

LUCIUS: *The strings, my lord, are poor.*

BRUTUS: *He thinks he still is at his instrument. Lucius, awake!*

LUCIUS: *My lord?*

BRUTUS: *Did you dream, Lucius, that you so cried out so?*

LUCIUS: *My lord, I don't know that I did cry.*

BRUTUS: *Yes, that you did. Did you see anything?*

LUCIUS: *Nothing, my lord.*

BRUTUS: *Sleep again, Lucius. Claudius!*
[To Varro.] Friend, awake!

VARRO: *My lord?*

CLAUDIUS: *My lord?*

169

BRUTUS: Why did you so cry out, sirs, in your sleep?

VARRO AND CLAUDIUS: Did we, my lord?

BRUTUS: Ay, saw you any thing?

350   VARRO: No, my lord, I saw nothing.

CLAUDIUS: Nor I, my lord.

BRUTUS: Go and commend me to my brother Cassius;
        Bid him set on his powers betimes before,
        And we will follow.

355   VARRO AND CLAUDIUS: It shall be done, my lord.   *[Exeunt.]*

BRUTUS: Why did you cry out so, sirs, in your sleep?

VARRO AND CLAUDIUS: Did we, my lord?

BRUTUS: Yes. Did you see anything?

VARRO: No, my lord, I saw nothing.

CLAUDIUS: Nor I, my lord.

BRUTUS: Go and commend me to my brother Cassius. Ask him to lead his army early, and we will follow him.

VARRO AND CLAUDIUS: It will be done, my lord.   [Exit.]

ACT V

SCENE 1
The plains of Philippi.

[Enter Octavius, Antony, and their Army.]

OCTAVIUS: Now, Antony, our hopes are answered.
    You said the enemy would not come down,
    But keep the hills and upper regions.
    It proves not so. Their battles are at hand;
5   They mean to warn us at Philippi here,
    Answering before we do demand of them.

ANTONY: Tut, I am in their bosoms, and I know
    Wherefore they do it. They could be content
    To visit other places, and come down
10   With fearful bravery, thinking by this face
    To fasten in our thoughts that they have courage;
    But 'tis not so.

[Enter a Messenger.]

MESSALA: Prepare you, generals.
    The enemy comes on in gallant show;
15   Their bloody sign of battle is hung out,
    And something to be done immediately.

ANTONY: Octavius, lead your battle softly on,
    Upon the left hand of the even field.

ACT V

SCENE 1
The plains of Philippi.

[Enter Octavius, Antony, and their Army.]

OCTAVIUS: *Now, Antony, our hopes are indeed answered. You said that the enemy would not come down but instead keep to the hills and upper regions. It proves not to be so. Their battles are at hand; they mean to challenge us here at Philippi, answering our challenge before we do demand anything of them.*

ANTONY: *Bah, I know their hearts, and I know why they do it. They could be content to stay in other places. But they come down with a timid show of bravery, thinking by this deed that they will convince us of their courage. But it is not so.*

[Enter a Messenger.]

MESSALA: *Prepare yourselves, generals. The enemy comes on in a gallant show. Their bloody flag of battle is hung out, and something is to be done immediately.*

ANTONY: *Octavius, lead your men to the left side of this field.*

OCTAVIUS: Upon the right hand I, keep thou the left.

20   ANTONY: Why do you cross me in this exigent?

OCTAVIUS: I do not cross you, but I will do so.   *[March.]*

[Drum. Enter Brutus, Cassius, and their Army; Lucilius, Titinius, Messala, and others.]

BRUTUS: They stand, and would have parley.

CASSIUS: Stand fast, Titinius; we must out and talk.

OCTAVIUS: Mark Antony, shall we give sign of battle?

25   ANTONY: No, Caesar, we will answer on their charge.
        Make forth, the generals would have some words.

OCTAVIUS: Stir not until the signal.

BRUTUS: Words before blows. Is it so, countrymen?

OCTAVIUS: Not that we love words better, as you do.

30   BRUTUS: Good words are better than bad strokes, Octavius.

ANTONY: In your bad strokes, Brutus, you give good words.
        Witness the hole you made in Caesar's heart,
        Crying "Long live! Hail, Caesar!"

CASSIUS: Antony,
35   The posture of your blows are yet unknown;
        But for your words, they rob the Hybla bees,
        And leave them honeyless.

ANTONY: Not stingless too.

OCTAVIUS: *I will go to right side; you take the left.*

ANTONY: *Why do you cross me in this crisis?*

OCTAVIUS: *I do not cross you now, but I will do so.*

[As Anthony and Octavius prepare to leave, a drum sounds. Enter Brutus, Cassius, and their Army; Lucilius, Titinius, Messala, and others.]

BRUTUS: *They stand and would speak with us.*

CASSIUS: *Stand fast, Titinius; we must go out and talk to them.*

OCTAVIUS: *Mark Antony, should we begin the battle?*

ANTONY: *No, Caesar, we will go out to talk. Let's go; the generals would have some words.*

OCTAVIUS: [Turns and says to his generals.] *Do not stir until the signal.*

[Brutus, Octavius, Anthony, and Cassius meet center stage.]

BRUTUS: *Words should come before blows. Is it not so, countrymen?*

OCTAVIUS: *Not that we love words better, as you do Brutus.*

BRUTUS: *Good words are still better than bad strokes, Octavius.*

ANTONY: *In your bad strokes, Brutus, you give good words. See the hole you made in Caesar's heart while crying, "Long live! Hail, Caesar!"*

CASSIUS: *Antony, how you will fight is unknown; but your words certainly could rob the bees of their honey since they are so sweet.*

ANTONY: *I am not stingless, either.*

BRUTUS: O, yes, and soundless too,

40   For you have stol'n their buzzing, Antony,

     And very wisely threat before you sting.

ANTONY: Villains! You did not so when your vile daggers

     Hack'd one another in the sides of Caesar.

     You show'd your teeth like apes, and fawn'd like hounds,

45   And bow'd like bondmen, kissing Caesar's feet;

     Whilst damned Casca, like a cur, behind

     Struck Caesar on the neck. O you flatterers!

CASSIUS: Flatterers? Now, Brutus, thank yourself.

     This tongue had not offended so today,

50   If Cassius might have ruled.

OCTAVIUS: Come, come, the cause. If arguing make us sweat,

     The proof of it will turn to redder drops.

     Look, I draw a sword against conspirators;

     When think you that the sword goes up again?

55   Never, till Caesar's three and thirty wounds

     Be well avenged, or till another Caesar

     Have added slaughter to the sword of traitors.

BRUTUS: Caesar, thou canst not die by traitors' hands,

     Unless thou bring'st them with thee.

60   OCTAVIUS: So I hope,

     I was not born to die on Brutus' sword.

BRUTUS: O, if thou wert the noblest of thy strain,

     Young man, thou couldst not die more honorable.

CASSIUS: A peevish school boy, worthless of such honor,

65   Join'd with a masker and a reveller!

ANTONY: Old Cassius still!

BRUTUS: *Yes, nor soundless too. You have also stolen their buzzing, Antony, and very wisely threaten before you sting.*

ANTONY: *Villains, you did not do so before your vile daggers plunged into the sides of Caesar. You showed your teeth like apes and fawned like pets and bowed like slaves, kissing Caesar's feet, while damned Casca, like a dog, struck Caesar from behind in the neck. You false flatterers!*

CASSIUS: *Flatterers? Now, Brutus, thank yourself for this. Antony would not have offended you today, if Cassius had had his way with Antony earlier.*

OCTAVIUS: *Well, what do you want? This arguing makes us sweat; we will answer you with blood. Look, I draw a sword against conspirators. When do you think that the sword will be put away again? Never, until Caesar's thirty-three wounds are avenged or until another Caesar has been slaughtered by the swords of traitors.*

BRUTUS: *Caesar, you cannot die by traitors' hands unless you bring those hands here.*

OCTAVIUS: *So I hope I was not born to die on Brutus' sword.*

BRUTUS: *If you were the noblest of your family, young man, you could not die more honorably.*

CASSIUS: *You, Octavius, are a nasty schoolboy, worthless of such honor, joined to a masker and a reveler!*

ANTONY: *The same old Cassius!*

OCTAVIUS: Come, Antony, away!
    Defiance, traitors, hurl we in your teeth.
    If you dare fight today, come to the field;
70   If not, when you have stomachs.
                     [Exeunt Octavius, Antony, and their Army.]

CASSIUS: Why, now, blow and, swell billow, and swim bark!
    The storm is up, and all is on the hazard.

BRUTUS: Ho, Lucilius! Hark, a word with you.

LUCILIUS: *[Stands forth.]* My lord?
                   [Brutus and Lucilius converse apart.]

75   CASSIUS: Messala!

MESSALA: [Stands forth.] What says my general?

CASSIUS: Messala,
    This is my birthday, as this very day
    Was Cassius born. Give me thy hand, Messala.
80   Be thou my witness that, against my will,
    As Pompey was, am I compell'd to set
    Upon one battle all our liberties.
    You know that I held Epicurus strong,
    And his opinion. Now I change my mind,
85   And partly credit things that do presage.
    Coming from Sardis, on our former ensign
    Two mighty eagles fell, and there they perch'd,
    Gorging and feeding from our soldiers' hands,
    Who to Philippi here consorted us.
90   This morning are they fled away and gone,
    And in their steads do ravens, crows, and kites
    Fly o'er our heads and downward look on us,
    As we were sickly prey. Their shadows seem
    A canopy most fatal, under which
95   Our army lies, ready to give up the ghost.

Octavius: Come, Antony, let us leave! We hurl defiance at you. If you dare fight today, come to the field; if not, come when you have the stomachs for it.

[Exit Octavius, Antony, and their Army.]

Cassius: Why, now, blow wind. Let the tempest begin! The storm is up, and all is on the line.

Brutus: Wait, Lucilius! Please, a word with you.

Lucilius: My lord?

[Lucilius and Brutus move to side and speak.]

Cassius: Messala!

Messala: [Comes forward.] What does my general say?

Cassius: Messala, this is my birthday. Give me your hand, Messala. Be my witness that, against my will I am forced to risk all our liberties upon one battle, just as Pompey was. You know that I always believed in Epicurus' philosophy. Now I change my mind, and give some credence to omens. Coming from Sardis, two mighty eagles dove down and perched on our former banner. They gorged and fed from the hands of soldiers who have come with us to Philippi. This morning the eagles flew away; and instead we see ravens, crows, and kites. They fly over our heads and look down on us as if we were their prey. Their shadows loom large and seem to foreshadow our army's doom.

MESSALA: Believe not so.

CASSIUS: I but believe it partly,
    For I am fresh of spirit and resolved
    To meet all perils very constantly.

100 BRUTUS: Even so, Lucilius.

CASSIUS: Now, most noble Brutus,
    The gods today stand friendly, that we may,
    Lovers in peace, lead on our days to age!
    But, since the affairs of men rest still incertain,
105   Let's reason with the worst that may befall.
    If we do lose this battle, then is this
    The very last time we shall speak together.
    What are you then determined to do?

110 BRUTUS: Even by the rule of that philosophy
    By which I did blame Cato for the death
    Which he did give himself: I know not how,
    But I do find it cowardly and vile,
    For fear of what might fall, so to prevent
115   The time of life: arming myself with patience
    To stay the providence of some high powers
    That govern us below.

CASSIUS: Then, if we lose this battle,
    You are contented to be led in triumph
120   Thorough the streets of Rome?

BRUTUS: No, Cassius, no. Think not, thou noble Roman,
    That ever Brutus will go bound to Rome;
    He bears too great a mind. But this same day
    Must end that work the ides of March begun.
125   And whether we shall meet again I know not.
    Therefore our everlasting farewell take.
    For ever, and for ever, farewell, Cassius!

MESSALA: Do not believe it.

CASSIUS: I only believe it partly. I am fresh of spirit and resolved to meet all perils in a determined way.

BRUTUS: Even so, Lucilius.

[Lucilius exits; Brutus and Cassius to center stage.]

CASSIUS: Now, most noble Brutus, the gods today stand by our side so that we may live long, peaceful lives! But, since the affairs of men are always uncertain, let's reason what the worst is that might happen to us. If we lose this battle, then this is the very last time we will speak together. What are you determined to do?

BRUTUS: The stoics preach that suicide is cowardly, and I find it very wicked to do what Cato did to himself. Think it cowardly to kill oneself for fear of what might happen; rather, arming myself with patience, I wait the end that the gods have destined us for.

CASSIUS: Then, if we lose this battle, you will accept being led in triumph through the streets of Rome?

BRUTUS: No, Cassius, no. Don't think that Brutus will ever go bound to Rome. I bear too great a mind. But this very day must end the work that was begun on the fifteenth of March. Whether we shall meet again, I know not. Therefore, let us take our everlasting farewell. Forever and forever farewell, Cassius! If we do meet again, why, we shall smile; if not, why then this parting was well made.

If we do meet again, why, we shall smile;
If not, why then this parting was well made.

130 CASSIUS: For ever and for ever farewell, Brutus!
If we do meet again, we'll smile indeed;
If not, 'tis true this parting was well made.

BRUTUS: Why then, lead on. O, that a man might know
The end of this day's business ere it come!
135 But it sufficeth that the day will end,
And then the end is known. Come, ho! Away!

[Exeunt.]

SCENE 2
The field of battle.

[Alarum. Enter Brutus and Messala.]

BRUTUS: Ride, ride, Messala, ride, and give these bills
Unto the legions on the other side. [Loud alarum.]
Let them set on at once, for I perceive
But cold demeanor in Octavius' wing,
5 And sudden push gives them the overthrow.
Ride, ride, Messala. Let them all come down.

[Exeunt.]

CASSIUS: *Forever and forever farewell, Brutus! If we do meet again, we'll smile indeed; if not, it is true that this parting was well made.*

BRUTUS: *Why then, lead on. That a man might know the end of a day's business before it comes! But it is sufficient that the day will end, and then the end will be known. Come, let's go!*
[Exit.]

SCENE 2
The field of battle.

[Sounds of battle, enter Brutus and Messala.]

BRUTUS: *Ride, ride, Messala, ride. Give these instructions to the legions on the other side.* [Loud alarm.]
Let them move at once. I notice a lack of fervor in Octavius' troops, and a sudden push will overthrow them. Ride, ride, Messala. Let them all come down. [Exit.]

183

SCENE 3
Another part of the field.

[Alarums. Enter Cassius and Titinius.]

CASSIUS: O, look, Titinius, look, the villains fly!
Myself have to mine own turn'd enemy.
This ensign here of mine was turning back;
I slew the coward, and did take it from him.

5   TITINIUS: O Cassius, Brutus gave the word too early,
Who, having some advantage on Octavius,
Took it too eagerly. His soldiers fell to spoil,
Whilst we by Antony are all enclosed.

[Enter Pindarus.]

10   PINDARUS: Fly further off, my lord, fly further off;
Mark Antony is in your tents, my lord;
Fly, therefore, noble Cassius, fly far off.

CASSIUS: This hill is far enough. Look, look, Titinius:
Are those my tents where I perceive the fire?

15   TITINIUS: They are, my lord.

CASSIUS: Titinius, if thou lovest me,
Mount thou my horse and hide thy spurs in him,
Till he have brought thee up to yonder troops
And here again, that I may rest assured
20   Whether yond troops are friend or enemy.

TITINIUS: I will be here again, even with a thought.   *[Exit.]*

CASSIUS: Go, Pindarus, get higher on that hill;
My sight was ever thick; regard Titinius,
And tell me what thou notest about the field.

184

SCENE 3
Another part of the field.

[Sounds of battle, enter Cassius and Titinius.]

CASSIUS: *Look, Titinius, look! The villains fly! I myself have to become an enemy to my own troops. This flag bearer here of mine was running away. I slew the coward and took the flag from him.*

TITINIUS: *Cassius, Brutus gave the order too early. Having some advantage on Octavius, he took it too quickly; his soldiers fell to looting while we are surrounded by Antony.*

[Enter Pindarus.]

PINDARUS: *Flee, my lord; fly further off. Mark Antony is in your tents, my lord. Fly, therefore, noble Cassius, fly far off.*

CASSIUS: *This hill is far enough from the main battle. Look, look, Titinius. Are those my tents which are on fire?*

TITINIUS: *They are, my lord.*

CASSIUS: *Titinius, if you care for me, mount my horse and dig in your spurs until he has brought you to those troops over there. Return here so that I may rest assured whether they are friend or enemy.*

TITINIUS: *I will be here again as quickly as a thought.*   [Exit.]

CASSIUS: *Go, Pindarus, get higher on that hill. My sight isn't very good. Watch Titinius, and tell me what you see.*

[Pindarus ascends the hill.]

25   This day I breathed first: time is come round,
     And where I did begin, there shall I end;
     My life is run his compass. Sirrah, what news?

PINDARUS: *[Above.]* O my lord!

CASSIUS: What news?

30   PINDARUS: *[Above.]* Titinius is enclosed round about
     With horsemen, that make to him on the spur;
     Yet he spurs on. Now they are almost on him.
     Now, Titinius! Now some light. O, he lights too.
     He's ta'en [Shout.] And, hark! They shout for joy.

35   CASSIUS: Come down; behold no more.
     O, coward that I am, to live so long,
     To see my best friend ta'en before my face!
     [Pindarus descends.]
     Come hither, sirrah.
     In Parthia did I take thee prisoner,
40   And then I swore thee, saving of thy life,
     That whatsoever I did bid thee do,
     Thou shouldst attempt it. Come now, keep thine oath;
     Now be a freeman, and with this good sword,
     That ran through Caesar's bowels, search this bosom.
45   Stand not to answer: here, take thou the hilts;
     And when my face is cover'd, as 'tis now,
     Guide thou the sword. *[Pindarus stabs him.]*
                         Caesar, thou art revenged,
     Even with the sword that kill'd thee.   *[Dies.]*

50   PINDARUS: So, I am free, yet would not so have been,
     Durst I have done my will. O Cassius!
     Far from this country Pindarus shall run,
     Where never Roman shall take note of him.
                                         [Exit.]

[Pindarus ascends the hill.]

This day began with my first breath. Now time has come full circle. I am where I did begin; there shall I end. My life has run its course. Sir, what news?

PINDARUS: [Above.] *Oh, my lord!*

CASSIUS: *What news?*

PINDARUS: [Above.] *Titinius is surrounded with horsemen who close towards him quickly. Yet he spurs on. Now they are almost on him. Quick, Titinius! Now some get off their horses. He does too. He's taken.* [Shout.] *And, listen! They shout for joy.*

CASSIUS: *Come down. Watch no more. I am a coward to live so long as to see my best friend taken before my face!*
[Pindarus descends.]

Come here, sir. In Parthia I took you prisoner, and I made you swear that, whatsoever I did bid you do, you should attempt it. Come now, and keep your oath; be a freeman, and with this good sword which ran through Caesar's bowels, find my chest. Don't question this. Here. Take the hilt; and when my face is covered, guide the sword to my chest. [Pindarus stabs him.] *Caesar, you are revenged with the same sword that killed you.* [Cassius Dies.]

PINDARUS: *So, I am free. Yet, I would not have it so if I had done my own will. Cassius, Pindarus will run far from this country to where no Roman can take notice of him.* [Exit.]

[Re-enter Titinius with Messala.]

MESSALA: It is but change, Titinius, for Octavius
55   Is overthrown by noble Brutus' power,
        As Cassius' legions are by Antony.

TITINIUS: These tidings would well comfort Cassius.

MESSALA: Where did you leave him?

TITINIUS: All disconsolate,
60   With Pindarus his bondman, on this hill.

MESSALA: Is not that he that lies upon the ground?

TITINIUS: He lies not like the living. O my heart!

MESSALA: Is not that he?

TITINIUS: No, this was he, Messala,
65   But Cassius is no more. O setting sun,
        As in thy red rays thou dost sink to night,
        So in his red blood Cassius' day is set,
        The sun of Rome is set! Our day is gone;
        Clouds, dews, and dangers come; our deeds are done!
70   Mistrust of my success hath done this deed.

MESSALA: Mistrust of good success hath done this deed.
        O hateful error, melancholy's child,
        Why dost thou show to the apt thoughts of men
        The things that are not? O error, soon conceived,
75   Thou never comest unto a happy birth,
        But kill'st the mother that engender'd thee!

TITINIUS: What, Pindarus! Where art thou, Pindarus?

MESSALA: Seek him, Titinius, whilst I go to meet
        The noble Brutus, thrusting this report

[Re-enter Titinius with Messala.]

MESSALA: *It is but an exchange, Titinius. Octavius is overthrown by noble Brutus' army as Cassius' legions are by Antony's.*

TITINIUS: *These tidings would well comfort Cassius.*

MESSALA: *Where did you leave him?*

TITINIUS: *All upset, with Pindarus his slave upon this hill.*

MESSALA: *Is that not he who lies upon the ground?*

TITINIUS: *He lies not like the living. Oh, my heart!*

MESSALA: *Is that not he?*

TITINIUS: *No, this was he, Messala; but Cassius is no more. Just as the setting sun sinks with red rays tonight, likewise Cassius' day is set in his red blood. The sun of Rome is set! Our day has gone. Clouds, dews, and dangers come; our deeds are done! Mistrust of my success has done this deed.*

MESSALA: *Fear of failure has done this deed. Wicked error, child of sadness, why do you show men the things that are not? Error, conceived in haste, is never a happy birth, but instead kills the mother who gives it birth!*

TITINIUS: *Hello, Pindarus! Where are you, Pindarus?*

MESSALA: *Seek him, Titinius, while I go to meet the noble Brutus, thrusting this report into his ears. I may say thrusting it, for piercing steel and poi-*

80 Into his ears. I may say "thrusting" it,
    For piercing steel and darts envenomed
    Shall be as welcome to the ears of Brutus
    As tidings of this sight.

    TITINIUS: Hie you, Messala,
85 And I will seek for Pindarus the while.   *[Exit Messala.]*
    Why didst thou send me forth, brave Cassius?
    Did I not meet thy friends? And did not they
    Put on my brows this wreath of victory,
    And bid me give it thee? Didst thou not hear their shouts?
90 Alas, thou hast misconstrued every thing!
    But, hold thee, take this garland on thy brow;
    Thy Brutus bid me give it thee, and I
    Will do his bidding. Brutus, come apace,
    And see how I regarded Caius Cassius.
95 By your leave, gods, this is a Roman's part.
    Come, Cassius' sword, and find Titinius' heart.

                                    [Kills himself.]

[Alarum. Re-enter Messala, with Brutus, young Cato, and others.]

BRUTUS: Where, where, Messala, doth his body lie?

MESSALA: Lo, yonder, and Titinius mourning it.

BRUTUS: Titinius' face is upward.

100 CATO: He is slain.

BRUTUS: O Julius Caesar, thou art mighty yet!
    Thy spirit walks abroad, and turns our swords
    In our own proper entrails.   *[Low alarums.]*

    CATO: Brave Titinius!
105 Look whether he have not crown'd dead Cassius!

soned darts would be as welcome to the ears of Brutus as news of this sight.

TITINIUS: *Leave, Messala, and I will seek out Pindarus.*   [Exit Messala.]

Why did you send me away, brave Cassius? Did I not meet your friends? Did they not put on my brows this wreath of victory, and bid me give it to you? Did you not hear their shouts? Alas, you have misunderstood everything! I place this garland on your brow. Brutus told me to give it to you, and I will do his bidding. Brutus, come quickly and see how I regarded Caius Cassius. By your leave, gods—this is a Roman's role. Come, Cassius' sword and find Titinius' heart.
[Kills himself.]

[Sounds of battle, re-enter Messala, with Brutus, young Cato, and others.]

BRUTUS: *Where? Where, Messala, does his body lie?*

MESSALA: *It lies over there with Titinius mourning it.*

BRUTUS: *Titinius' face is turned upward.*

CATO: *He is slain.*

BRUTUS: *Oh, Julius Caesar, you are still mighty! Your spirit walks abroad and turns our swords towards our own stomachs.*   [Low alarums.]

CATO: *Brave Titinius! Look where he has crowned dead Cassius!*

191

BRUTUS: Are yet two Romans living such as these?
　　　The last of all the Romans, fare thee well!
　　　It is impossible that ever Rome
　　　Should breed thy fellow. Friends, I owe moe tears
110　　To this dead man than you shall see me pay.
　　　I shall find time, Cassius, I shall find time.
　　　Come therefore, and to Thasos send his body;
　　　His funerals shall not be in our camp,
　　　Lest it discomfort us. Lucilius, come,
115　　And come, young Cato; let us to the field.
　　　Labeo and Flavius, set our battles on.
　　　'Tis three o'clock, and Romans, yet ere night
　　　We shall try fortune in a second fight.　　*[Exeunt.]*

SCENE 4
Another part of the field.

[Alarum. Enter, fighting, Soldiers of both armies; then Brutus, young Cato, Lucilius, and others.]

BRUTUS: Yet, countrymen, O, yet hold up your heads!　　*[Exit.]*

CATO:　What bastard doth not? Who will go with me?
　　　I will proclaim my name about the field.
　　　I am the son of Marcus Cato, ho!
5　　　A foe to tyrants, and my country's friend.
　　　I am the son of Marcus Cato, ho!

BRUTUS: And I am Brutus, Marcus Brutus, I;
　　　Brutus, my country's friend; know me for Brutus!
　　　　　　　　　　　　　　[Young Cato is slain.]

LUCILIUS: O young and noble Cato, art thou down?
10　　Why, now thou diest as bravely as Titinius,
　　　And mayst be honor'd, being Cato's son.

ACT V SCENE 4

BRUTUS: *Are there two Romans yet living such as these? The last of all the true Romans, farewell! It is impossible that ever Rome should breed your equal. Friends, I owe more tears to this dead man than I ever can repay. I shall find time, Cassius; I shall find time. Come, therefore, and send his body to Thasos. His funerals will not be in our camp; it might upset us. Lucilius, come, and come, young Cato; let us go to the field. Labio and Flavio, begin our battles again. It is only three o'clock; and Romans, we will try our luck in a second battle before nightfall.*

[Exit.]

SCENE 4
Another part of the field.

[Sounds of battle. Enter, fighting, Soldiers of both armies; then Brutus, young Cato, Lucilius, and others.]

BRUTUS: *Countrymen, still hold up your heads!*   [Exit.]

CATO: *What bastard does not? Who will go with me? I will proclaim my name about the field. I am the son of Marcus Cato, a foe to tyrants and my country's friend. I am the son of Marcus Cato.*

[Enter soldiers and fight.]

BRUTUS: *And I am Brutus—Marcus Brutus. Brutus, my country's friend. Know that I am Brutus!*   [Exit.]

LUCILIUS: *Young and noble Cato, are you down? Why, now you die as bravely as Titinius did and may you be honored as Cato's son.*

193

First Soldier: Yield, or thou diest.

Lucilius: Only I yield to die.   *[Offers money.]*
     There is so much that thou wilt kill me straight:
15   Kill Brutus, and be honor'd in his death.

First Soldier: We must not. A noble prisoner!

Second Soldier: Room, ho! Tell Antony, Brutus is ta'en.

First Soldier: I'll tell the news. Here comes the general.

[Enter Antony.]
     Brutus is ta'en, Brutus is ta'en, my lord.

20   Antony: Where is he?

Lucilius: Safe, Antony, Brutus is safe enough.
     I dare assure thee that no enemy
     Shall ever take alive the noble Brutus;
     The gods defend him from so great a shame!
25   When you do find him, or alive or dead,
     He will be found like Brutus, like himself.

Antony: This is not Brutus, friend, but, I assure you,
     A prize no less in worth. Keep this man safe,
     Give him all kindness; I had rather have
30   Such men my friends than enemies. Go on,
     And see whether Brutus be alive or dead,
     And bring us word unto Octavius' tent
     How every thing is chanced.   *[Exeunt.]*

FIRST SOLDIER: *Yield, or you die.*

LUCILIUS: *I yield only to death; [Offers money.] there is so much money here that you will kill me immediately. Kill Brutus, and be honored by his death.*

FIRST SOLDIER: *We must not. He makes a noble prisoner!*

SECOND SOLDIER: *Make room, here! Tell Antony that Brutus is captured.*

FIRST SOLDIER: *I'll tell him the news. Here comes the general.*

[Enter Antony.]
Brutus is taken; Brutus is captured, my lord.

ANTONY: *Where is he?*

LUCILIUS: *Safe, Antony. Brutus is safe enough. I promise you that no enemy will ever take the noble Brutus alive. May the gods defend him from so great a shame! When you do find him, alive or dead, he will be found like Brutus, like himself.*

ANTONY: *This is not Brutus, friend; but, I assure you he is a prize no less in worth. Keep this man safe; give him kindnesses. I would rather have such men as my friends than as my enemies. Go on, and see whether Brutus is alive or dead. Bring word to Octavius' tent how everything has played out.* [Exit.]

SCENE 5
Another part of the field.

[Enter Brutus, Dardanius, Clitus, Strato, and Volumnius.]

BRUTUS: Come, poor remains of friends, rest on this rock.

CLITUS: Statilius show'd the torch-light, but, my lord,
  He came not back. He is or ta'en or slain.

BRUTUS: Sit thee down, Clitus. Slaying is the word:
5   It is a deed in fashion. Hark thee, Clitus.   *[Whispers.]*

CLITUS: What, I, my lord? No, not for all the world.

BRUTUS: Peace then, no words.

CLITUS: I'll rather kill myself.

BRUTUS: Hark thee, Dardanius.   *[Whispers.]*

10   DARDANIUS: Shall I do such a deed?

CLITUS: O Dardanius!

DARDANIUS: O Clitus!

CLITUS: What ill request did Brutus make to thee?

DARDANIUS: To kill him, Clitus. Look, he meditates.

15   CLITUS: Now is that noble vessel full of grief,
    That it runs over even at his eyes.

BRUTUS: Come hither, good Volumnius, list a word.

VOLUMNIUS: What says my lord?

SCENE 5
Another part of the field.

[Enter Brutus, Dardanius, Clitus, Strato, and Volumnius.]

BRUTUS: *Come, friends, let us rest on this rock.*

CLITUS: *Statilius showed our way with the torch; but, my lord, he did not come back. He has been either captured or slain.*

BRUTUS: *Sit down, Clitus. Slaying is the proper word. Indeed, it is in fashion. Listen, Clitus.*   [Brutus whispers to him.]

CLITUS: *What, I, my lord? No, not for all the world.*

BRUTUS: *Quiet then! No words.*

CLITUS: *I would rather kill myself.*

BRUTUS: *Listen, Dardanius.*   [Brutus whispers.]

DARDANIUS: *How would I do such a deed?*

CLITUS: *Oh, Dardanius!*

DARDANIUS: *Oh, Clitus!*

CLITUS: *What ill request did Brutus make of you?*

DARDANIUS: *To kill him, Clitus. Look, he meditates.*

CLITUS: *Now that noble vessel is so full of grief that it runs over even at his eyes.*

BRUTUS: *Come here, good Volumnius, listen to a word.*

VOLUMNIUS: *What says my lord?*

BRUTUS: Why, this, Volumnius:
20   The ghost of Caesar hath appear'd to me
         Two several times by night; at Sardis once,
         And this last night here in Philippi fields.
         I know my hour is come.

VOLUMNIUS: Not so, my lord.

25   BRUTUS: Nay, I am sure it is, Volumnius.
         Thou seest the world, Volumnius, how it goes;
         Our enemies have beat us to the pit; *[Low alarums.]*
         It is more worthy to leap in ourselves
         Than tarry till they push us. Good Volumnius,
30   Thou know'st that we two went to school together;
         Even for that our love of old, I prithee,
         Hold thou my sword-hilts, whilst I run on it.

VOLUMNIUS: That's not an office for a friend, my lord.
                                              [Alarum still.]

CLITUS: Fly, fly, my lord, there is no tarrying here.

35   BRUTUS: Farewell to you, and you, and you, Volumnius.
         Strato, thou hast been all this while asleep;
         Farewell to thee too, Strato. Countrymen,
         My heart doth joy that yet in all my life
         I found no man but he was true to me.
40   I shall have glory by this losing day,
         More than Octavius and Mark Antony
         By this vile conquest shall attain unto.
         So, fare you well at once, for Brutus' tongue
         Hath almost ended his life's history.
45   Night hangs upon mine eyes, my bones would rest
         That have but labor'd to attain this hour.
                         [Alarum. Cry within, "Fly, fly, fly!"]

CLITUS: Fly, my lord, fly.

BRUTUS: Why, only this, Volumnius. The ghost of Caesar has appeared to me several times by night. Once at Sardis, and then last night here in Philippi's fields. I know my hour of death comes.

VOLUMNIUS: Not so, my lord.

BRUTUS: No. I am sure it is, Volumnius. You see the world, Volumnius, how it goes; our enemies have driven us to a hole.   [Low alarums.]
It is more worthy to leap in ourselves than stay until they push us in. Good Volumnius, you know that we two went to school together. Especially for our old loyalty, I pray, hold my sword's hilt while I run onto it.

VOLUMNIUS: That's not an office for a friend, my lord.

[Alarum still.]

CLITUS: Fly, fly, my lord; there is no staying here.

BRUTUS: Farewell to you, and you, and you, Volumnius. Strato, you have been all this while asleep; farewell to you too, Strato. Countrymen, my heart is happy with the fact that in all my life I didn't find a single man who was disloyal to me. I shall have more glory in this losing day— more than Octavius and Mark Antony will have by their vile conquest. So, fare you well, for Brutus' tongue has almost said his last. Night hangs upon my eyes; my bones would rest that have labored so hard to meet this hour.

[Alarum. Cry within, "Fly, fly, fly!"]

CLITUS: Fly, my lord, fly.

BRUTUS: Hence! I will follow.
                [Exeunt Clitus, Dardanius, and Volumnius.]
      I prithee, Strato, stay thou by thy lord.
50   Thou art a fellow of a good respect;
      Thy life hath had some smatch of honor in it.
      Hold then my sword, and turn away thy face,
      While I do run upon it. Wilt thou, Strato?

STRATO: Give me your hand first. Fare you well, my lord.

55   BRUTUS: Farewell, good Strato. *[Runs on his sword.]*
      Caesar, now be still;
      I kill'd not thee with half so good a will.   *[Dies.]*

[Alarum. Retreat. Enter Octavius, Antony, Messala, Lucilius, and the Army.]

OCTAVIUS: What man is that?

MESSALA: My master's man. Strato, where is thy master?

60   STRATO: Free from the bondage you are in, Messala:
      The conquerors can but make a fire of him;
      For Brutus only overcame himself,
      And no man else hath honor by his death.

LUCILIUS: So Brutus should be found. I thank thee, Brutus,
      That thou hast proved Lucilius' saying true.

65   OCTAVIUS: All that served Brutus, I will entertain them.
      Fellow, wilt thou bestow thy time with me?

STRATO: Ay, if Messala will prefer me to you.

OCTAVIUS: Do so, good Messala.

MESSALA: How died my master, Strato?

BRUTUS: *Away! I will follow.*   [Exit Clitus, Dardanius, and Volumnius.]
  I pray, Strato, stay by your lord. You are a well-respected man. Your life
  smacks of honor. Hold my sword, and turn away your face while I run
  upon it. Will you, Strato?

STRATO: *Give me your hand first. Farewell, my lord.*

BRUTUS: *Farewell, good Strato.* [Runs on his sword.] *Caesar, now be still.*
  I didn't kill you as willingly as I do kill myself. [Dies.]

[Alarum. Retreat. Enter Octavius, Antony, Messala, Lucilius, and the
Army.]

OCTAVIUS: *What man is that?*

MESSALA: *My master's servant. Strato, where is your master, Brutus?*

STRATO: *Free from the bondage you are in, Messala. The conquerors can*
  make only a funeral pyre for him. Brutus overcame himself, and no other
  man will gain honor by his death.

LUCILIUS: *This is how Brutus should be found. I thank you, Brutus, for prov-*
  ing what I predicted to be true.

OCTAVIUS: *All who served Brutus may join us. Fellow, will you spend your*
  time with me?

STRATO: *Yes, if Messala will direct me to you.*

OCTAVIUS: *Do so, good Messala.*

MESSALA: *How died my master, Strato?*

70   STRATO: I held the sword, and he did run on it.

      MESSALA: Octavius, then take him to follow thee
         That did the latest service to my master.

      ANTONY: This was the noblest Roman of them all.
         All the conspirators, save only he,
75   Did that they did in envy of great Caesar;
         He only, in a general honest thought
         And common good to all, made one of them.
         His life was gentle, and the elements
         So mix'd in him that Nature might stand up
80   And say to all the world, "This was a man!"

      OCTAVIUS: According to his virtue let us use him
         With all respect and rites of burial.
         Within my tent his bones tonight shall lie,
         Most like a soldier, order'd honorably.
85   So call the field to rest, and let's away,
         To part the glories of this happy day.

                                          [Exeunt.]

                          THE END

STRATO: *I held the sword, and he did run on it.*

MESSALA: *Octavius, then take him to follow you since he performed the last service to my master.*

ANTONY: *This was the noblest Roman of them all. All the conspirators other than he, did what they did in envy of great Caesar. Only Brutus had a general honest thought and common good in mind. His life was gentle and the elements so mixed in him that Nature might stand up and say to all the world, "This was a man!"*

OCTAVIUS: *Because of his virtue, let us honor him with all respect and rites of burial. Tonight within my tent his bones will lie like a soldier, ordered honorably. Call the army to rest; let's leave to divide the glories of this happy day.* [Exit.]

THE END

STUDY GUIDE

Act I, Scene 1 - A Street (Flavius, Marullus, and commoners)

1. Puns and word-play are a popular part of Shakespeare's plays. Explain the punning and word-play in which the cobbler engages.

2. How do the Tribunes, Marullus and Flavius, react to this word-play?

3. Why do they chase the commoners away, and with what do they rebuke them?

4. What do they suggest the commoners do?

5. Why do Marullus and Flavius seem to fear Caesar?

Act I, Scene 2 - Rome, The Same (Caesar, Antony, Calpurnia, Brutus, Cassius, Casca, a Soothsayer, and others)

1. What does Caesar say to Antony in front of everyone? What does it say about Caesar? What does Antony's response say about him?

2. What is the Soothsayer's warning to Caesar? What does it mean?

3. When they are alone, what accusation does Cassius make to Brutus? What is Brutus' response?

4. What point is Cassius making when he asks Brutus about seeing his [Brutus' own] face? What does he propose he will do?

5. On what fear of Brutus' does Cassius pick up?

6. How does Brutus explain to Cassuis what he means by this fear.

7. According to Cassius, what happens when he and Caesar go swimming in the Tiber? What is the point of this story?

8. Why does Cassius refer to Caesar as "a sick girl"? How would you describe Cassius at this point?

9. What does Cassius say about fate, free will, and being underlings?

10. After delaying an answer, what is Brutus' conclusion about his own feelings on freedom?

11. As the scene continues, what does Caesar say to Antony about Cassius? What is Antony's response?

12. What does Caesar's response about fear show about him?

13. According to Casca, what does Antony offer Caesar three times? What is Caesar's response?

14. What two physical ailments of Caesar are mentioned in this scene?

15. In response to the "falling sickness," what is the meaning of Cassius' sarcasm?

16. What happens to Marullus and Flavius? Why?

17. What action will Cassius take to get Brutus to join the conspirators?

18. After Brutus leaves, how is Cassius brutally honest with himself?

Act I, Scene 3 - Rome; A Street (Casca, Cicero, Cinna, and Cassius)

1. What is Cassius' interpretation of the night's strange events?

2. On whom does Cassius blame Caesar's power?

3. Why does Casca say he is no "fleering telltale"?

4. Why is it important to the conspirators to have Brutus come on their side?

Act II, Scene 1 - Brutus' House (Brutus, Cassius, Portia, Lucius, Ligarius, and others)

1. Why does Brutus believe that Caesar must be stopped from becoming king? Do you think Brutus' fear of what Caesar may become is justified?

2. Brutus receives the messages planted by Cassius, and seems inclined to take action to stop Caesar. What does Brutus tell the audience about his mental/emotional state at this point?

3. What does Cassius suggest the conspirators do that Brutus disagrees with? Why does Brutus disagree?

4. What does the conspirators' discussion about Cicero reveal about the group?

5.   Cassius recognizes that Antony should die, too, but Brutus says no. Why?

6.   There is some concern that Caesar, having grown superstitious lately, might not leave the house the next day. How does Decius say he can manipulate Caesar? What does this say about Caesar's personality?

7.   What is Brutus' answer when Portia asks why he has been behaving strangely lately? What is her response to this?

8.   What action has Portia taken to sway Brutus to confide in her?

Act II, Scene 2 - Caesar's House (Caesar, Calpurnia, Decius, Brutus, and others)

1.   What does Calpurnia cry out in her sleep?

2.   What does Calpurnia say to prove her point that the evening's strange events relate to Caesar and not to the world in general?

3.   The priests "augurers" offer an animal to the gods. What in their examination suggests to them that Caesar should not leave his house?

4.   What is Decius' interpretation of Calpurnia's bloody dream?

5.   What, according to Decius, might some of the senators conclude if Caesar refuses to come to the capitol today?

6.   What is the sad irony in Caesar's perception of all those who come to his house?

Act II, Scene 3 - A Street Near the Capitol (Artemidorus)

1. Why is Artemidorus waiting for Caesar?

Act II, Scene 4 - Another Part of the Same Street Near Brutus' House (Portia, Lucius, and the Soothsayer)

1. What order does Portia give Lucius? Why is she so unsettled?

2. In this scene, how is Portia different from the Portia we see earlier?

Act III, Scene 1 - Rome: before the Capitol, the Senate Steps (Caesar, Brutus, Antony, Cassius, the Soothsayer, Artemidorus, and others)

1. Why does Caesar say he will not read Artemidorus' letter first? How is this part of the posture he has taken?

2. What does Trebonius do while Popilius Lena speaks to Caesar?

3. In his response to Cimber's request to lift his brother's banishment, what posture does Caesar assume?

4. After all the conspirators stab Caesar, Brutus does too. What is Caesar's comment after Brutus stabs him, and what does it say about Caesar's perception of friendship?

5. After stabbing Caesar, the conspirators prepare for an attack from Caesar's friends. What does Brutus say about death?

6.   What does Brutus suggest they do before going to the marketplace? Why?

7.   In a message, Antony states that he will be supportive of Brutus only if Brutus does what?

8.   Why does Antony not seem angry with Caesar's murderers?

9.   What conditions are placed on Antony if he is to speak at Caesar's funeral?

10. After all exit, Antony reveals his true intentions in his famous soliloquy. What are his intentions?

11. What message does Antony want Octavius' servant to take to Octavius?

Act III, Scene 2 - Rome: the Forum (Brutus, Cassius, Antony, and citizens of Rome)

1.   What is Brutus' answer to any man who might wonder why he killed Caesar?

2.   What is the crowd's reaction to Brutus' speech?

3.   What line about Brutus in Antony's oration is repeated so often that its meaning becomes ironic?

4.   What piece of paper does Antony claim to have?

5.   How does Antony describe the stab wound Brutus gave Caesar?

6.   In his speech, Antony claims to lack what talent?

7.   What does the reaction of the mob indicate?

Act III, Scene 3 - Rome; a Street (Cinna, the poet, and a mob)

1.   Why is Cinna, the poet, killed by the mob?

Act IV, Scene 1 - Rome: a Room in Antony's House (Antony, Octavius, and Lepidus)

1.   How does Antony, who has been thought of as a man who spends his time drinking and chasing women, show himself to be ruthless in this scene?

2.   Why do you think Octavius assents to Antony's suggestion regarding Lepidus?

3.   In what unfavorable terms does Antony describe Lepidus, and what do these lines reveal about Antony and Octavius' plan?

Act IV, Scene 2 - Before Brutus' Tent: a camp in Turkey, near Sardis. (Brutus, Titinius, Lucius, Pindarus, and Cassius)

1.   Of whom is Brutus speaking when he says, "Thou hast described a hot friend cooling"?

2.   Why does Brutus suggest that he and Cassius hold their discussion inside the tent?

Act IV, Scene 3 - Brutus' Tent (Brutus, Cassius, and others)

1. For what reason does Brutus claim that Cassius is often condemned by the people?

2. Why is Brutus so outraged at official corruption?

3. How does Cassius try to intimidate Brutus?

4. What is Brutus' response?

5. In speaking of honesty, why does Brutus sound immodest?

6. Brutus says that he is too honest to get money to pay his soldiers by dishonest means; so he goes to Cassius for the money, and Cassius denies him the money. Since Brutus knows Cassius gets money dishonestly, how can Brutus go to Cassius for money?

7. What is the point and tone of Cassius' speech in response to Brutus?

8. After the poet interrupts and speaks of "Love and be friends," what do we find is a cause for Brutus' grief?

9. What is the difference between Brutus' and Cassius' plans for engaging the armies of Antony and Octavius?

10. The lines about "taking action" are famous lines. What is their meaning?

Act V, Scene 1 - The Plains of Philippi

1. What does Antony think is the reason for Brutus' and Cassius' armies having confronted them face to face?

2. What is Octavius' response when Antony orders him to take the left side of the field? Why do you suppose Antony does this?

3. What does Cassius remark about Antony?

4. What do the ravens and crows flying overhead mean to Cassius?

5. What does Brutus say he finds "cowardly and vile"?

6. Brutus says he bears "too great a mind" to allow what to happen?

7. Why do Brutus and Cassius give each other an everlasting farewell?

8. Cassius reaffirms their friendship and leaves. Brutus sits down to read while Lucius plays soothing music. Then, what "monstrous apparition" does Brutus see and what message does it give him?

Act V, Scene 2 - The Field of Battle (Brutus and Messala)

1. What message is Messala ordered to take to "the legions on the other side"?

Act V, Scene 3 - Another Part of the Field (Cassius, Titinius, Pindarus, Messala, and Brutus)

1. According to Titinius, why is Cassius' side losing to Antony's forces?

2. How does Cassius die? Why?

3. It turns out that Cassius has killed himself prematurely. Why?

Act V, Scene 4 - Another Part of the Battlefield (Brutus, Cato, Lucilius, Antony, and others)

1. Who impersonates Brutus? Why?

Act V, Scene 5 - Another Part of the Battlefield (Brutus, Antony, Octavius, and others)

1. What do Clitus, Dardinius, and Volumnius refuse to do for Brutus that Strato does do for him?

2. As he dies, why does Brutus say, "Caesar, now be still"?

3. How do Antony and Octavius treat Brutus' body?